JUDGES

ORDINARY PEOPLE, EXTRAORDINARY GOD

WOODROW KROLL

CROSSWAY BOOKS

A PUBLISHING MINISTRY OF
GOOD NEWS PUBLISHERS
WHEATON, ILLINOIS

CH		16	15	14	13	12	11	10	09	08	07	06
15	14	13	12	11	10	9	8	7	6	5	4	3	2	1

Table of Contents

How to Use This Study

Your study of the judges will have maximum impact if you prayerfully read each day's Scripture passage. The relevant text of Judges and 1 Samuel from the English Standard Version is printed before each lesson's reading, so that everything you need is in one place. While we recommend reading the Scripture passage before you read the devotional, some have found it helpful to use the devotional as preparation for reading the Scripture. If you are unfamiliar with the English Standard Version (on which this series of studies is based), you might consider reading the selection, then the devotional, followed by reading the passage again from a different Bible text with which you are more comfortable. This will give you an excellent basis for considering the rest of the lesson.

With each devotional there are three sections designed to help you better understand and apply the lesson's Scripture passage.

Consider It—Several questions will help you unpack and reflect on the Scripture passage of the day. These could be used for a small group discussion.

Express It—Suggestions for turning the insights from the lesson into prayer.

Go Deeper—It is important to see each part of the Bible in the context of other passages and insights from Scripture. This brief section will allow you to consider some of the implications of the day's passage for the central theme of the study (Ordinary People, Extraordinary God) as well as the way it fits with the rest of Scripture.

Lesson

1

Partial Obedience, Complete Failure

The Book of Joshua (right before Judges) ends with Israel taking possession of the land God promised to them. But they only partially obeyed God's command. We'll begin our study by focusing on how Israel failed to do all God commanded and how partial obedience in our own lives can lead to complete disobedience later on.

Judges 1:1–3:6

The Continuing Conquest of Canaan

1 After the death of Joshua, the people of Israel inquired of the Lord, "Who shall go up first for us against the Canaanites, to fight against them?" ²The Lord said, "Judah shall go up; behold, I have given the land into his hand." ³And Judah said to Simeon his brother, "Come up with me into the territory allotted to me, that we may fight against the Canaanites. And I likewise will go with you into the territory allotted to you." So Simeon went with him. ⁴Then Judah went up and the Lord gave the Canaanites and the Perizzites into their hand, and they defeated 10,000 of them at Bezek. ⁵They found Adoni-bezek at Bezek and fought against him and defeated the Canaanites and the Perizzites. ⁶Adoni-bezek fled, but they pursued him and caught him and cut off his thumbs and his big toes. ⁷And Adoni-bezek said, "Seventy kings with their thumbs and their big toes cut off used to pick up scraps under my table. As I have done, so God has repaid me." And they brought him to Jerusalem, and he died there.

⁸And the men of Judah fought against Jerusalem and captured it and struck it with the edge of the sword and set the city on fire. ⁹And afterward the men of Judah went down to fight against the Canaanites who lived in the hill country, in the Negeb, and in the lowland. ¹⁰And Judah went against the Canaanites who lived in Hebron (now the name of Hebron was formerly Kiriath-arba), and they defeated Sheshai and Ahiman and Talmai.

¹¹From there they went against the inhabitants of Debir. The name of Debir was formerly Kiriath-sepher. ¹²And Caleb said, "He who attacks Kiriath-sepher and captures it, I will give him Achsah my daughter for a wife." ¹³And Othniel the son of Kenaz, Caleb's younger brother, captured it. And he gave him Achsah his daughter for a wife. ¹⁴When she came to him, she urged him to ask her father for a field. And she dismounted from her donkey, and Caleb said to her, "What do you want?" ¹⁵She said to him, "Give me a blessing. Since you have set me in the land of the Negeb, give me also springs of water." And Caleb gave her the upper springs and the lower springs.

¹⁶And the descendants of the Kenite, Moses' father-in-law, went up with the people of Judah from the city of palms into the wilderness of Judah, which lies in the Negeb near Arad, and they went and settled with the people. ¹⁷And Judah went with Simeon his brother, and they defeated the Canaanites who inhabited Zephath and devoted it to destruction. So the name of the city was called Hormah. ¹⁸Judah also captured Gaza with its territory, and Ashkelon with its territory, and Ekron with its territory. ¹⁹And the Lord was with Judah, and he took possession of the hill country, but he could not drive out the inhabitants of the plain because they had chariots of iron. ²⁰And Hebron was given to Caleb, as Moses had said. And he drove out from it the three sons of Anak. ²¹But the people of Benjamin did not drive out the Jebusites who lived in Jerusalem, so the Jebusites have lived with the people of Benjamin in Jerusalem to this day.

²²The house of Joseph also went up against Bethel, and the Lord was with them. ²³And the house of Joseph scouted out Bethel. (Now the name of the city was formerly Luz.) ²⁴And the spies saw a man coming out of the city, and they said to him, "Please show us the way into the city,

and we will deal kindly with you." ²⁵And he showed them the way into the city. And they struck the city with the edge of the sword, but they let the man and all his family go. ²⁶And the man went to the land of the Hittites and built a city and called its name Luz. That is its name to this day.

Failure to Complete the Conquest

²⁷Manasseh did not drive out the inhabitants of Beth-shean and its villages, or Taanach and its villages, or the inhabitants of Dor and its villages, or the inhabitants of Ibleam and its villages, or the inhabitants of Megiddo and its villages, for the Canaanites persisted in dwelling in that land. ²⁸When Israel grew strong, they put the Canaanites to forced labor, but did not drive them out completely.

²⁹And Ephraim did not drive out the Canaanites who lived in Gezer, so the Canaanites lived in Gezer among them.

³⁰Zebulun did not drive out the inhabitants of Kitron, or the inhabitants of Nahalol, so the Canaanites lived among them, but became subject to forced labor.

³¹Asher did not drive out the inhabitants of Acco, or the inhabitants of Sidon or of Ahlab or of Achzib or of Helbah or of Aphik or of Rehob, ³²so the Asherites lived among the Canaanites, the inhabitants of the land, for they did not drive them out.

³³Naphtali did not drive out the inhabitants of Beth-shemesh, or the inhabitants of Beth-anath, so they lived among the Canaanites, the inhabitants of the land. Nevertheless, the inhabitants of Beth-shemesh and of Beth-anath became subject to forced labor for them.

³⁴The Amorites pressed the people of Dan back into the hill country, for they did not allow them to come down to the plain. ³⁵The Amorites persisted in dwelling in Mount Heres, in Aijalon, and in Shaalbim, but the hand of the house of Joseph rested heavily on them, and they became subject to forced labor. ³⁶And the border of the Amorites ran from the ascent of Akrabbim, from Sela and upward.

Israel's Disobedience

2 Now the angel of the Lord went up from Gilgal to Bochim. And he said, "I brought you up from Egypt and brought you into the land that I swore to give to your fathers. I said, 'I will never break my covenant with you, ²and you shall make no covenant with the inhabitants of this land; you shall break down their altars.' But you have not obeyed my voice. What is this you have done? ³So now I say, I will not drive them out before you, but they shall become thorns in your sides, and their gods shall be a snare to you." ⁴As soon as the angel of the Lord spoke these words to all the people of Israel, the people lifted up their voices and wept. ⁵And they called the name of that place Bochim. And they sacrificed there to the Lord.

The Death of Joshua

⁶When Joshua dismissed the people, the people of Israel went each to his inheritance to take possession of the land. ⁷And the people served the Lord all the days of Joshua, and all the days of the elders who outlived Joshua, who had seen all the great work that the Lord had done for Israel. ⁸And Joshua the son of Nun, the servant of the Lord, died at the age of 110 years. ⁹And they buried him within the boundaries of his inheritance in Timnath-heres, in the hill country of Ephraim, north of the mountain of Gaash. ¹⁰And all that generation also were gathered to their fathers. And there arose another generation after them who did not know the Lord or the work that he had done for Israel.

Israel's Unfaithfulness

¹¹And the people of Israel did what was evil in the sight of the LORD and served the Baals. ¹²And they abandoned the LORD, the God of their fathers, who had brought them out of the land of Egypt. They went after other gods, from among the gods of the peoples who were around them, and bowed down to them. And they provoked the LORD to anger. ¹³They abandoned the LORD and served the Baals and the Ashtaroth. ¹⁴So the anger of the LORD was kindled against Israel, and he gave them over to plunderers, who plundered them. And he sold them into the hand of their surrounding enemies, so that they could no longer withstand their enemies. ¹⁵Whenever they marched out, the hand of the LORD was against them for harm, as the LORD had warned, and as the LORD had sworn to them. And they were in terrible distress.

Key Verse

"So now I say, I will not drive them out before you, but they shall become thorns in your sides, and their gods shall be a snare to you" (Judg. 2:3).

The LORD Raises Up Judges

¹⁶Then the LORD raised up judges, who saved them out of the hand of those who plundered them. ¹⁷Yet they did not listen to their judges, for they whored after other gods and bowed down to them. They soon turned aside from the way in which their fathers had walked, who had obeyed the commandments of the LORD, and they did not do so. ¹⁸Whenever the LORD raised up judges for them, the LORD was with the judge, and he saved them from the hand of their enemies all the days of the judge. For the LORD was moved to pity by their groaning because of those who afflicted and oppressed them. ¹⁹But whenever the judge died, they turned back and were more corrupt than their fathers, going after other gods, serving them and bowing down to them. They did not drop any of their practices or their stubborn ways. ²⁰So the anger of the LORD was kindled against Israel, and he said, "Because this people have transgressed my covenant that I commanded their fathers and have not obeyed my voice, ²¹I will no longer drive out before them any of the nations that Joshua left when he died, ²²in order to test Israel by them, whether they will take care to walk in the way of the LORD as their fathers did, or not." ²³So the LORD left those nations, not driving them out quickly, and he did not give them into the hand of Joshua.

3 Now these are the nations that the LORD left, to test Israel by them, that is, all in Israel who had not experienced all the wars in Canaan. ²It was only in order that the generations of the people of Israel might know war, to teach war to those who had not known it before. ³These are the nations: the five lords of the Philistines and all the Canaanites and the Sidonians and the Hivites who lived on Mount Lebanon, from Mount Baal-hermon as far as Lebo-hamath. ⁴They were for the testing of Israel, to know whether Israel would obey the commandments of the LORD, which he commanded their fathers by the hand of Moses. ⁵So the people of Israel lived among the Canaanites, the Hittites, the Amorites, the Perizzites, the Hivites, and the Jebusites. ⁶And their daughters they took to themselves for wives, and their own daughters they gave to their sons, and they served their gods.

Go Deeper

Judges 1:19 goes by so fast, it's easy to miss. Look at the last half of the verse: "but he [the tribe of Judah] could not drive out the inhabitants of the plain because they had chariots of iron." It doesn't seem very significant at first. But when you consider that chariots of iron on broad plains are a formidable weapon, it makes sense that Judah let them be.

This only highlights a problem that will become all too familiar. The Israelites left God out of the equation. Look back at Joshua 17:18. Here Joshua reminds the people that "you shall drive out the Canaanites, though they have chariots of iron, and though they are strong." Why was he so confident? He had seen the power of God at work.

Not too long before this, Joshua and the people of Israel had seen the walls of Jericho fall. The generations before had seen the Red Sea part and swallow an army. What stopped Judah in 1:19 wasn't the strength of their enemy; it was the loss of their trust in God.

The same is true today. The apostle Paul reminds us that "we are more than conquerors through him [Jesus] who loved us" (Rom. 8:37). Do you believe that? If you do, nothing will stop you from completing the purpose God has for you.

I f you picked up this study thinking you'd learn about such popular judges as Judge Judy or the judges of the Supreme Court, then you've come to the wrong place. The judges discussed here faced the same type of situations you and I do in everyday life. Looking at the way they met those challenges will help us meet our own. Seeing where they failed will help us avoid the same mistakes.

First, we need to understand the difference between contemporary judges and biblical judges. Today, our judges sit in the courtroom listening to disputes brought before them by lawyers representing two sides of a case. The judge's job is to make sure the case is presented lawfully and to make judgments based on the law. And while some of our judges are in very influential positions, none of them rise to the same level that the biblical judges did.

If today's judges hand out judgments, many of the judges in this book actually *carried out* judgments. The judges were often military leaders who rallied the people to war against foreign armies. Even Deborah, the only woman judge mentioned in the Old Testament, was involved in a great military victory. (See Judg. 4:4–5.)

So, if the biblical judges carried out judgments, *whose* judgments did they carry out? The answer—God's. During this period of about 300 years, the Israelites fell under almost constant attack. Among Israel's many enemies were the Midianites from the south, the Canaanites from the north and Moabites and Ammonites from the east. The judges were God's instruments for driving these invaders out.

Historically, the land of Israel has always been a military hotspot. It occupies a strategic and productive place in what is often called "the crossroads of the world." But the Bible goes into greater detail as to why Israel fell under attack so often. "They abandoned the LORD and served the Baals and the Ashtaroth. So the anger of the LORD was kindled against Israel, and he gave them over to plunderers, who plundered them. And he sold them into the hand of their surrounding enemies" (2:13–14).

Hold on a minute! God gave them over to their enemies? This may fly in the face of many popular ideas about who God is and how He acts, but it's right here in the Bible. God allowed foreign enemies to attack Israel, His people, the people He made a covenant (promise) with to give them this land as an eternal inheritance. (See Genesis 15.) There must be a reason.

"They abandoned the LORD and served the Baals and the Ashtaroth" (Judg. 2:13). To understand why this was such a big deal, imagine how a man might feel after finding out that his wife of many years has been seeing other men. By worshiping the foreign gods, Israel was turning their back on God who had loved and provided so much for them. Baal and Ashtaroth represented the gods of the people who lived in the Promised Land before Israel got there. They were about as opposite from the true living God as you could imagine, encouraging all sorts of sexual immorality and violent acts.

While God, out of His anger, sent the foreign enemies, there's more to it than that. Too often people read Judges and

> " *Too often people read Judges and see only a God of wrath, yet they completely overlook the God of love and mercy.* "

see only a God of wrath (wrath is present, make no mistake), yet they completely overlook the God of love and mercy. The judges themselves were a sign that God still loved Israel. "Whenever the LORD raised up judges for them, the LORD was with the judge, and he saved them from the hand of their enemies all the days of the judge. For the LORD was moved to pity by their groaning because of those who afflicted and oppressed them" (2:18).

The enemies were a way of calling Israel back to God. They would be an object lesson in the results and consequences of sin. Unfortunately this process—serving foreign gods, being subdued, crying out to God and being rescued—is actually the beginning of a cycle that repeats itself at least seven times in the book of Judges.

The same cycle is repeated on a personal level in the lives of Christians even today. But by looking at the lives of the judges God raised up, we'll learn the lessons we need to break out of that cycle and always live in the blessing of God.

Express It

Maybe your ideas of God and His nature have been challenged already. Maybe you're having a hard time reconciling the anger of God with the love of God. Pray today that God would help you understand how seriously He takes sin. Ask Him to reassure you that everything He does is ultimately motivated by love and a desire to restore the relationship that sin has destroyed.

Consider It

As you read Judges 1:1–3:6, consider these questions:

1) What is the common theme in 1:27–36?

2) Instead of driving out the people, what compromise do some of the Israelites make?

3) How could things have been different if Israel had driven out all the nations of Canaan?

4) What is God asking you to drive out of your life?

5) How does Judges 2:10 describe the generation that rose after Joshua?

6) What might be a reason for this?

7) How did the people respond when told that God would no longer drive out the Canaanite nations?

8) Why does God say He'll leave the enemy nations in Canaan?

Othniel—Who Will Go Up?

Othniel, the first judge of Israel, was a man of strength and courage who fought fearlessly for the Lord. Through this lesson, we'll see that success comes not just from personal strength but from our trust in God as well.

Judges 3:7–11

Othniel

⁷And the people of Israel did what was evil in the sight of the LORD. They forgot the LORD their God and served the Baals and the Asheroth. ⁸Therefore the anger of the LORD was kindled against Israel, and he sold them into the hand of Cushan-rishathaim king of Mesopotamia. And the people of Israel served Cushan-rishathaim eight years. ⁹But when the people of Israel cried out to the LORD, the Lord raised up a deliverer for the people of Israel, who saved them, Othniel the son of Kenaz, Caleb's younger brother. ¹⁰The Spirit of the LORD was upon him, and he judged Israel. He went out to war, and the LORD gave Cushan-rishathaim king of Mesopotamia into his hand. And his hand prevailed over Cushan-rishathaim. ¹¹So the land had rest forty years. Then Othniel the son of Kenaz died.

> # Key Verse
>
> *The Spirit of the LORD was upon him, and he judged Israel. He went out to war, and the LORD gave Cushan-rishathaim king of Mesopotamia into his hand* (Judg. 3:10).

Go Deeper

In Judges 3:11 we read, "So the land had rest forty years. Then Othniel the son of Kenaz died." Did Othniel know the importance of the fight against Cushan-rishathaim? Did he realize that this one battle would usher in peace for just one generation?

Maybe not, but even if the result had been only 40 days of peace, the fight would have been worth it. Today God's enemies take the form of immoral lifestyles and selfish decisions in our daily lives. Instead of seeing an army of invaders threatening to take our life, we see an army of propaganda and worldly lies threatening to draw us from the very Source of life.

Not all enemies are for us to fight, but God has a calling for you. And whether you change things for a nation or for just one person, the fight is worth it.

I f you were to list all the biblical judges you know, who would first come to mind? Probably Samson with his incredible strength. Or Gideon whose army of 300 men won a might victory. Perhaps you'll think of Deborah the woman warrior. But what about Othniel?

If you read your Bible straight through from beginning to end, you might know that this isn't the first time we meet Othniel. We are first introduced to this future judge of Israel back in Joshua 15.

"And Caleb said, 'Whoever strikes Kiriath-sepher and captures it, to him will I give Achsah my daughter as wife.' And Othniel the son of Kenaz, the brother of Caleb, captured it" (Josh. 15:16–17).

Now that's a résumé for a judge! First of all, Othniel knew how to fight. Kiriath-sepher was one of the Canaanite strongholds in the Promised Land and would be a hard city to take. But Othniel rose to the challenge, and the city fell.

Next, notice who Othniel's uncle is: Caleb. This is the same Caleb who stood alone with Joshua and declared, "Let us go up at once and occupy it, for we are well able to overcome it" (Num. 13:30), when Israel was too afraid to enter the Promised Land. God Himself described Caleb as a "servant . . . [who] has followed me fully" (Num. 14:24). Caleb led many battles in the conquest of the Promised Land and remained a faithful servant of God to the end. That's a family history to be proud of.

So, not only was Othniel a proven warrior and a man with a proud family heritage, he was a devoted servant of God. That's evident from the days he led Israel as a judge.

Remember, many of the judges were military leaders raised up by God to lead the people and drive out the foreign enemies. God allowed these enemies to menace Israel when the people turned from Him to worship the idols of the surrounding pagan nations. This disciplinary action wouldn't have been necessary if Israel had remembered that God commanded them to drive out *all* the existing nations in the Promised Land. Israel didn't, and as a result, the people of Israel were pulled away from God by the pagan practices of the Canaanites left behind. God knew that if all the pagan nations were not driven out, a situation like that of Judges 3:6–7 would arise:

"And their daughters they took to themselves for wives, and their own daughters they gave to their sons, and they served their gods. And the people of Israel did what was evil in the sight of the LORD. They forgot the LORD their God and served the Baals and the Asheroth."

The enemy God brought in was Cushan-rishathaim (his name means "doubly wicked"), king of Mesopotamia (modern Iraq). And after eight years, the people of Israel had enough and cried out to God for help. God called on Othniel, and "the Spirit of the LORD was upon him, and he judged Israel. He went out to war" (3:10).

Though Othniel was the man who led the battle, the real hero of this story is God. God heard the cry of Israel, God raised up Othniel (v. 9), God's Spirit came on Othniel and God gave the foreign army into Othniel's hand (v. 10).

Notice, too, how God used Othniel. It was in a very straightforward way that played to Othniel's strengths. There were no surprises here. He had fought many battles and stood up for the Lord before; this time was no different.

God doesn't always call us out of our comfort zones to serve Him. For as many people as He calls to live as missionaries in a foreign land, there are those He calls to serve Him right where they are with what they do best.

What are the talents, skills, and abilities you have? Are you making yourself usable to God with them?

Express It

Sometimes people get so caught up in expecting God to call them elsewhere they forget to serve Him where they are. As you pray, ask God to show you how you can serve Him where you are today. Praise Him for the abilities He's given you, and thank Him for the opportunity to use those abilities to make His name known.

Consider It

As you read Judges 3:7–11, consider these questions:

1) **What does God hate about the Canaanite gods?**

   _____

   _____

   _____

2) **What are things today that could be considered idols?**

   _____

   _____

   _____

3) **How do you think God feels about the idols we entertain today?**

   _____

   _____

   _____

4) **Are there any ungodly influences you've allowed to stand in your life?**

   _____

   _____

   _____

5) **What do these verses tell you about how God deals with sin?**

   _____

   _____

   _____

6) **What are the areas where God has made you strong?**

   _____

   _____

   _____

7) **What ways can you use those strengths for God?**

   _____

   _____

   _____

Lesson
3

Ehud—Things Aren't as They Seem

Ehud, the second judge of Israel, was one of the last people you'd expect God to use. He was left-handed and quite possibly disabled. But in looking at Ehud's example, we'll see that the only prerequisite for service in God's kingdom is a heart ready and willing to be used in any way.

Judges 3:12–30

Ehud

¹²And the people of Israel again did what was evil in the sight of the LORD, and the LORD strengthened Eglon the king of Moab against Israel, because they had done what was evil in the sight of the LORD. ¹³He gathered to himself the Ammonites and the Amalekites, and went and defeated Israel. And they took possession of the city of palms. ¹⁴And the people of Israel served Eglon the king of Moab eighteen years.

¹⁵Then the people of Israel cried out to the LORD, and the LORD raised up for them a deliverer, Ehud, the son of Gera, the Benjaminite, left-handed man. The people of Israel sent tribute by him to Eglon the king of Moab. ¹⁶And Ehud made for himself a sword with two edges, a cubit in length, and he bound it on his right thigh under his clothes. ¹⁷And he presented the tribute to Eglon king of Moab. Now Eglon was a very fat man. ¹⁸And when Ehud had finished presenting the tribute, he sent away the people who carried the tribute. ¹⁹But he himself turned back at the idols near Gilgal and said, "I have a secret message for you, O king." And he commanded, "Silence." And all his attendants went out from his presence. ²⁰And Ehud came to him as he was sitting alone in his cool roof chamber. And Ehud said, "I have a message from God for you." And he arose from his seat. ²¹And Ehud reached with his left hand, took the sword from his right thigh, and thrust it into his belly. ²²And the hilt also went in after the blade, and the fat closed over the blade, for he did not pull the sword out of his belly; and the dung came out. ²³Then Ehud went out into the porch and closed the doors of the roof chamber behind him and locked them.

> # Key Verse
>
> *When he [Ehud] arrived, he sounded the trumpet in the hill country of Ephraim. Then the people of Israel went down with him from the hill country, and he was their leader* (Judg. 3:27).

²⁴When he had gone, the servants came, and when they saw that the doors of the roof chamber were locked, they thought, "Surely he is relieving himself in the closet of the cool chamber." ²⁵And they waited till they were embarrassed. But when he still did not open the doors of the roof chamber, they took the key and opened them, and there lay their lord dead on the floor.

²⁶Ehud escaped while they delayed, and he passed beyond the idols and escaped to Seirah. ²⁷When he arrived, he sounded the trumpet in the hill country of Ephraim. Then the people of Israel went down with him from the hill country, and he was their leader. ²⁸And he said to them, "Follow after me, for the LORD has given your enemies the Moabites into your hand." So they went down after him and seized the fords of the Jordan against the Moabites and did not allow anyone to pass over. ²⁹And they killed at that time about 10,000 of the Moabites, all strong, able-bodied men; not a man escaped. ³⁰So Moab was subdued that day under the hand of Israel. And the land had rest for eighty years.

Go Deeper

Ehud is a classic example of turning a potential weakness into a powerful tool in the hands of God. In the New Testament, the apostle Paul takes this to the next level—he rejoiced in his weaknesses.

Paul, through struggling with what he called his "thorn," realized that rather than a disability, his weakness drove him to God. God reassured Paul, "My grace is sufficient for you, for my power is made perfect in weakness" (2 Cor. 12:9).

Paul realized the kind of ability that God is looking for has nothing to do with strength or weakness. Instead, God is looking for just one ability: avail*ability*.

Whatever you may think of your talents and abilities, have you considered offering them to God? There are tremendous opportunities out there to spread God's love, and He wants you to be a part of that. Don't limit yourself by only offering the things you're good at; allow God to take your weaknesses too.

Take a few moments to write down everything you know about the 1940s. Who were the presidents, what movies were released? How many states were in the union then? (Hint: it wasn't 50!) What was the political climate like? Were people happy with their president? Were the people optimistic about the future?

Having a hard time coming up with anything? Well, if you would have asked a friend of Ehud's about the days of Othniel, you'd get about the same response. It's been a total of 58 years between the time Othniel fought his battle and when Ehud takes center stage. A lot can happen in 58 years, and a lot can be forgotten.

What started this forgetfulness? There was a spiritual void. Judges 3:11 tells us that Othniel died, but it says nothing about another judge taking his place. Ideally, Israel shouldn't have needed another judge. The judges were military leaders God used to drive out the foreign armies oppressing Israel. And the foreign armies came when Israel turned away from God to the gods of the Canaanites.

What would have happened if Israel had gotten their act together after Othniel judged the Mesopotamians? Othniel would have died, but the people of Israel could have still remembered God. They could have followed the laws handed down from Moses. They could have continued the conquest of Canaan and driven out more of the corruptive influences. They could have continued to honor the true living God in their lives.

Living with God as their King, there would have been no need for God to bring in foreign armies, and no need to raise up another judge. In the best case scenario, the people of Israel wouldn't have needed judges, because each of them would have worshiped and loved God to the exclusion of all others.

But when Othniel died, the people forgot about God and again turned to foreign gods. This time the invading army came from Moab under the leadership of Eglon. For 18 years, he oppressed Israel from Jericho. As invader kings usually do, Eglon demanded a tribute—basically a steep tax—from the Israelites. The amount must have been quite large because it took several men to deliver the tribute. One of those men was Ehud.

We know only a little about Ehud. He was from the tribe of Benjamin, and he was left-handed. This may have been simple, everyday left-handedness, but the Hebrew word used here ('itter) indicates he might have been somehow disabled. Perhaps his right hand was malformed, or maybe it had been injured at some point. Whatever the case, this apparent weakness became his greatest advantage.

When the people of Israel called out for deliverance, God chose Ehud to serve as judge and deliverer. But God didn't use Ehud the same way He used Othniel. While God used the strengths He had given to Othniel, in Ehud's case God utilized what we would call his weakness.

Because Ehud delivered the tribute to the Moabites, he had access to the king. Because he was left-handed, the guards didn't consider him a threat. And even if they did check Ehud's left hip for a weapon (where a right-hander would draw from), they would have missed Ehud's double-edged sword on his right side.

> ❝*Thankfully God doesn't see us the same way we often see ourselves.*❞

All Ehud had to do is get Eglon alone. And when Eglon agreed to meet Ehud privately in his room, his fate was sealed. Ehud killed the king, escaped and called Israel to arms. As a result, Moab was driven out of Israel, and the land had peace for 80 years.

When Ehud looked in a mirror, did he see a great hero on the order of Othniel or Joshua? Probably not. But thankfully God doesn't see us the same way we often see ourselves. Sometimes God will use you like Othniel, in the area of your strength. But sometimes God will call you like Ehud and ask you to trust that if you give your weakness into His hands, He can change it into strength to be used for Him.

Maybe you're disappointed today that your talent isn't one of those "attractive" ones like singing or preaching; maybe you're unable to do certain things because of a disability. Well, for everything you think you can't do, there are many things God can and will do through you. As long as you have air in your lungs, you have the ability to be used by God. The question is, will you let Him?

Express It

If you've drifted away from God, ask Him to remind you of what brought you to Him in the first place. As a popular worship song says, "Turn your eyes upon Jesus," and in the process, the things of this world will "grow strangely dim." Let God know you're available to Him. Whether you think you have the ability or not, allow God to show you what He can do with a willing heart.

Consider It

As you read Judges 3:12–30, consider these questions:

1) In what ways can you show that God is the King of your life?

_____

_____

_____

2) Israel didn't turn from God in a single day. What could cause them to forget God over time?

_____

_____

_____

3) What ways can you counter this "gradual amnesia" in your own life?

_____

_____

_____

4) Do you find it easy or difficult to classify your strengths?

_____

_____

_____

5) According to verse 28, was it really Ehud who defeated the Moabites?

_____

_____

_____

6) What does this passage tell you about your abilities, great or small?

_____

_____

_____

7) What are some of your weaknesses? Can you see how they could be used as a strength?

_____

_____

_____

Shamgar—Using What's At Hand

We know very little about Shamgar, but what we do know is impressive. Although he was a farmer caught in an unexpected situation, he stood and fought with what was at hand. In this lesson, we'll see that unplanned attacks often reveal what we truly believe in our hearts. And we'll learn to put our trust in God today rather than to wait until it's too late.

Judges 3:31

Shamgar

³¹After him was Shamgar the son of Anath, who killed 600 of the Philistines with an oxgoad, and he also saved Israel.

Go Deeper

A parallel to Shamgar's situation may be found in Gospel of Matthew where we see Jesus sending out the 12 disciples. They were told to go and proclaim, "the kingdom of heaven is at hand" (Matt. 10:7). The disciples were instructed to take only what they had at that moment. "Acquire no gold nor silver nor copper for your belts, no bag for your journey, nor two tunics nor sandals nor a staff" (vv. 9–10).

The disciples were to be dependent on the people with whom they shared about God and Jesus. But more than that, Jesus was illustrating to them that anyone doing the work of God will be given everything they need for whatever situation.

For Shamgar, an oxgoad may not have seemed like much, but it was more than enough in the hands of God.

Today's key verse may only contain 22 words, but each word is important because this is all we know about the judge Shamgar.

One thing about Shamgar stands out right away. He wasn't an Israelite. Shamgar is not a Hebrew name, and his father's name, Anath, is also the name of one of the Canaanite gods.

Was Shamgar's family at one time an Israelite family, worshiping the one true God? Possibly, and if so, their story was hardly unique. As we saw in Judges 3, for a long time the Israelites had been intermarrying with the Canaanite people that were left behind, as well as worshiping their gods.

Moses had warned Israel about this years ago. Just before his death and Israel's entrance into Canaan, he reminded them of God's command to "make no covenant with them and show no mercy to them. You shall not intermarry with them" (Deut. 7:2–3). Besides not wanting Israel to worship idols, God explains that this command is because He considers Israel "a people holy to the LORD" (7:6).

Israel was to be a nation set apart from all other nations, to be unique and distinct from the pagan cultures surrounding them. They were to be a beacon for the true and living God among all the false gods in the land. Today, Christians are called to be holy ambassadors for the Lord, set apart for His work. We need to be careful of anything that will take away our distinctiveness.

Shamgar was also a farmer or laborer, indicated by his use of an oxgoad, a long wooden stick with a metal tip at one end and a blade at the other. It was used to drive the oxen that plowed the fields. It was a farm implement, hardly a weapon of war.

Because of this fact, it seems likely (and amazing) that Shamgar's defeat of 600 Philistines happened on one unexpected occasion and not over a long period of time. When the Philistines came, there was no time to organize resistance or call for help. It was do or die.

This passage gives us a fleeting mention of the Philistines. In the time of Shamgar, they were only beginning to become powerful enough to harass Israel. They lived in the southwest part of Israel in the land allotted to the tribes of Judah and Simeon.

So, what made Shamgar stand and fight the Philistines? We don't know. When Othniel attacked Cushan-rishathaim and his army, it was clear that the Spirit of God had come upon him. Othniel fought for the glory of God. When Ehud assassinated Eglon the king of Moab, he also did so in the name of God. With Shamgar, all we have is the little description "and he also saved Israel."

By all indications, Shamgar was a simple man in the wrong place at the wrong time. He didn't have the time to prepare an

> **" *Often when God uses us, He does it at a moment's notice, asking that we only use what we have at hand.* "**

attack like Ehud did, and he didn't have the battle savvy of Othniel. But despite his background, despite his position in life, when God called him to action, Shamgar put his whole heart into it. Instead of standing aside to let the Philistines pass, Shamgar grabbed what was at hand and made a stand for God.

It would be nice if God always announced how He planned to use us. But if you were told that 600 Philistines were about to walk through your field and you'd have to face them with only an oxgoad, would that make it easier? Sometimes ignorance is a mercy. Shamgar didn't have time to question his ability or even his authority to fight such a battle.

Often when God uses us, He does it at a moment's notice, asking that we only use what we have at hand. Like with Shamgar, these unexpected situations often bring out where our heart really lies—with God or with ourselves. If that day of testing comes, remember Philippians 4:13 and Paul's triumphant declaration, "I can do all things through him that strengthens me."

Express It

As we've seen in the lives of Othniel, Ehud, and Shamgar, God can and will use us in many ways. Our responsibility isn't to figure out how God can best use us—that's for God to decide. We need to focus on making ourselves usable—to have clean hands and a pure heart. Pray along with Psalm 139:23–24: "Search me, O God, and know my heart! Try me and know my thoughts! And see if there be any grievous way in me, and lead me in the way everlasting!"

Consider It

As you read Judges 3:12–30, consider these questions:

1) If you could only have 22 words written about you, what would they be?

2) What does it mean to live a distinctively Christian life?

3) What in our society would distract you (or hinder you) from the Christian life?

4) Though you can't prepare for the unexpected, how can you prepare your heart to be used by God?

Lesson 5

Deborah— Leadership in Action

During the time of the judges, it would have been unusual for a woman to be in a position of authority as Deborah was. Yet she can teach us many valuable lessons about being a spiritual leader. We'll see that every believer has been called to spiritual leadership whether it's on the front lines or behind the scenes.

Judges 4:1–24

Deborah and Barak

4 And the people of Israel again did what was evil in the sight of the LORD after Ehud died. ²And the LORD sold them into the hand of Jabin king of Canaan, who reigned in Hazor. The commander of his army was Sisera, who lived in Harosheth-hagoyim. ³Then the people of Israel cried out to the LORD for help, for he had 900 chariots of iron and he oppressed the people of Israel cruelly for twenty years.

⁴Now Deborah, a prophetess, the wife of Lappidoth, was judging Israel at that time. ⁵She used to sit under the palm of Deborah between Ramah and Bethel in the hill country of Ephraim, and the people of Israel came up to her for judgment. ⁶She sent and summoned Barak the son of Abinoam from Kedesh-naphtali and said to him, "Has not the LORD, the God of Israel, commanded you, 'Go, gather your men at Mount Tabor, taking 10,000 from the people of Naphtali and the people of Zebulun. ⁷And I will draw out Sisera, the general of Jabin's army, to meet you by the river Kishon with his chariots and his troops, and I will give him into your hand'?" ⁸Barak said to her, "If you will go with me, I will go, but if you will not go with me, I will not go." ⁹And she said, "I will surely go with you. Nevertheless, the road on which you are going will not lead to your glory, for the LORD will sell Sisera into the hand of a woman." Then Deborah arose and went with Barak to Kedesh. ¹⁰And Barak called out Zebulun and Naphtali to Kedesh. And 10,000 men went up at his heels, and Deborah went up with him.

¹¹Now Heber the Kenite had separated from the Kenites, the descendants of Hobab the father-in-law of Moses, and had pitched his tent as far away as the oak in Zaanannim, which is near Kedesh.

¹²When Sisera was told that Barak the son of Abinoam had gone up to Mount Tabor, ¹³Sisera called out all his chariots, 900 chariots of iron, and all the men who were with him, from Harosheth-hagoyim to the river Kishon. ¹⁴And Deborah said to Barak, "Up! For this is the day in which the LORD has given Sisera into your hand. Does not the LORD go out before you?" So Barak went down from Mount Tabor with 10,000 men following him. ¹⁵And the LORD routed Sisera and all his chariots and all his army before Barak by the edge of the sword. And Sisera got down from his chariot and fled away on foot. ¹⁶And Barak pursued the chariots and the army to Harosheth-hagoyim, and all the army of Sisera fell by the edge of the sword; not a man was left.

> # Key Verse
>
> *And Deborah said to Barak, "Up! For this is the day in which the LORD has given Sisera into your hand. Does not the LORD go out before you?"* (Judg. 4:14).

¹⁷But Sisera fled away on foot to the tent of Jael, the wife of Heber the Kenite, for there was peace between Jabin the king of Hazor and the house of Heber the Kenite. ¹⁸And Jael came out to meet Sisera and said to him, "Turn aside, my lord; turn aside to me; do not be afraid." So he turned aside to her into the tent, and she covered him with a rug. ¹⁹And he said to her, "Please give me a little water to drink, for I am thirsty." So she opened a skin of milk and gave him a drink and covered

him. [20]And he said to her, "Stand at the opening of the tent, and if any man comes and asks you, 'Is anyone here?' say, 'No.'" [21]But Jael the wife of Heber took a tent peg, and took a hammer in her hand. Then she went softly to him and drove the peg into his temple until it went down into the ground while he was lying fast asleep from weariness. So he died. [22]And behold, as Barak was pursuing Sisera, Jael went out to meet him and said to him, "Come, and I will show you the man whom you are seeking." So he went in to her tent, and there lay Sisera dead, with the tent peg in his temple.

[23]So on that day God subdued Jabin the king of Canaan before the people of Israel. [24]And the hand of the people of Israel pressed harder and harder against Jabin the king of Canaan, until they destroyed Jabin king of Canaan.

Go Deeper

When thinking of spiritual leadership, many people get hung up on the word "leadership." "I'm not leader material," they say. "There are others with better management and people skills than me." But, as we see from Deborah's example, being a spiritual leader isn't so much about leading as it is about demonstrating God's power in your life.

At the heart of his letter to the Romans, the apostle Paul explains exactly what it means to live a spiritual life. "Present your bodies as a living sacrifice, holy and acceptable to God" (Rom. 12:1).

Through the rest of the chapter, Paul explains what this means—that we all serve a purpose in the Body of Christ, that we've all been given gifts to use for God's glory.

Paul goes on to say: "Let love be genuine. Abhor what is evil; hold fast to what is good" (12:9). Being a true spiritual leader means being a true servant of God. It means allowing Him to use your life to show His love and mercy to people who haven't heard this good news yet.

As you think about your role in spiritual leadership, ask yourself, *How am I living my life for God's glory today?*

Sometimes God will call a specific person for a specific purpose to act at a specific time. But God calls all of us to live our lives in service to Him all the time. Though we are not all called like Othniel, Ehud or Shamgar, we *are* called to be like Deborah and live a life of spiritual leadership.

The beginning of chapter 4 gives us a scene that's become familiar even this early in Judges. "And the people of Israel again did what was evil in the sight of the LORD after Ehud died" (Judg. 4:1). The cycle begins *again*—a man of godly influence dies, and the people forget that it's up to them to walk in the ways of God. The fact that they turned away so quickly indicates their hearts weren't set on following God but on their earthly leader.

Well, most of them anyway. The first picture we have of Deborah is of her sitting under a palm tree settling the disputes people brought to her. While the function of biblical judges was often military, Deborah's role also resembles that of a modern-day judge. Though most of Israel had turned to the gods of Canaan, Deborah remained faithful to the Lord and even helped people to apply His law to their lives.

It's no wonder that God chose her when Israel cried out for deliverance. You see, God isn't looking for "couch potato" Christians to work for Him. Instead, God will use people who are available and already active in His service. If you're anxious for God to use you in big ways, get out there now and be useful in little ways.

When God let Deborah know He was ready to deliver Israel from Sisera, what she *didn't* do is as interesting as what she *did* do. She didn't strap on a sword and yell "charge!" Instead she called on Barak. This has nothing to do with the roles of women in the military. Rather, it merely reflects that Deborah recognized there was someone better to lead an attack. When the time came, Deborah didn't insist on leading. The deliverance of Israel from Sisera was more important to her than her own personal agenda.

When God calls us into action, He calls us to use all our resources. Often our greatest resources are the people God places in our lives. Delegating tasks can be difficult because we don't always like to share the credit for a job well done. But when it comes to fulfilling God's mission, only His glory is important.

Anyone who's ever been in charge of a team knows that some people need a little extra motivation. Deborah found that with Barak. Even though he was the right man for the job of driving out Sisera and his army, Barak needed a little persuasion. Deborah started by reminding him that God wasn't *suggesting* they drive out Sisera, He was *commanding* them.

Second, God had already promised they would be victorious. "And I will draw out Sisera . . . with his chariots and his troops, and I will give him into your hand" (4:7). It's hard to seriously object to God's call when He's promised such an outcome.

Finally, Deborah agreed to go with Barak. Whether Barak was uncertain of his leadership abilities or if he was wise enough to realize that the people would more likely follow him if they knew Deborah was involved, Barak asked for her assistance. A leader like Deborah knows when she's needed to give assistance. She didn't go grudgingly or complaining; she just went.

The result of all this was an amazing victory against incredible odds. Sisera's army had 900 iron chariots. If you remember chapter 1, the people of Judah left many Canaanites alone because they didn't want to face their superior weaponry. Deborah and Barak prove that when fighting God's fight, it's not about the strength of the enemy but about our trust in God.

Spiritual leadership isn't reserved only for certain members of society. Everyone who has trusted Jesus as their Savior is called to be a leader. But being a spiritual leader doesn't necessarily mean being in a position of authority, though it certainly can. Being a spiritual leader is really more about being a "spiritual demonstrator." Demonstrating a life lived wholly for the Lord is something we are all called to do.

Express It

The concept of leadership scares some people and exhilarates others. Regardless of where you stand, ask God to help you find your role in His kingdom. Ask for His help in living a godly life. If there are certain habits or a lifestyle you need to get rid of in order to do this, pray that God would help you unseat these "enemies."

Consider It

As you read Judges 4:1–24, consider these questions:

1) Israel was under Sisera's control for 20 years. Why might it have taken so long for Israel to reach the breaking point?

2) What, if any, "enemy" influences do you allow to stay in your life?

3) What reasons do you have for not getting rid of these influences?

4) Based on God's response to Israel when they cried out for help, how will He respond to you?

5) Though Barak seemed a little uncertain about the battle, what was the outcome?

6) Are you in a position of leadership? What lessons can you learn from Deborah?

7) Are you in a "follower" position? Have your thoughts on spiritual leadership changed? Stayed the same? How?

Lesson
6

Deborah— Responding in Praise

Even though Barak led the fight against Sisera's army and Jael dealt the killing blow, Deborah knew that the victory was God's alone. By looking at the song of Deborah, we will learn to give thanks to God always—something that can be too easily forgotten.

Judges 5:1–31

The Song of Deborah and Barak

5 Then sang Deborah and Barak the son of Abinoam on that day:

2"That the leaders took the lead in Israel,
   that the people offered themselves
      willingly,
   bless the LORD!
3"Hear, O kings; give ear, O princes;
   to the LORD I will sing;
   I will make melody to the LORD, the God
      of Israel.
4"LORD, when you went out from Seir,
   when you marched from the region of
      Edom,
the earth trembled
   and the heavens dropped,
   yes, the clouds dropped water.
5The mountains quaked before the LORD,
   even Sinai before the LORD, the God of
      Israel.
6"In the days of Shamgar, son of Anath,
   in the days of Jael, the highways were
      abandoned,
   and travelers kept to the byways.
7The villagers ceased in Israel;
   they ceased to be until I arose;
   I, Deborah, arose as a mother in
      Israel.
8When new gods were chosen,
   then war was in the gates.
Was shield or spear to be seen
   among forty thousand in Israel?
9My heart goes out to the commanders of
      Israel
   who offered themselves willingly among
      the people
   Bless the LORD.
10"Tell of it, you who ride on white
      donkeys,
   you who sit on rich carpets
   and you who walk by the way.
11To the sound of musicians at the
      watering places,
   there they repeat the righteous triumphs
      of the LORD,

> # Key Verse
>
> *"Hear, O kings; give ear, O princes; to the LORD I will sing; I will make melody to the LORD, the God of Israel"* (Judg. 5:3).

---

the righteous triumphs of his villagers in
      Israel.
"Then down to the gates marched the
      people of the LORD.
12"Awake, awake, Deborah!
   Awake, awake, break out in a song!
Arise, Barak, lead away your captives,
   O son of Abinoam.
13Then down marched the remnant of the
      noble;
   the people of the LORD marched down for
      me against the mighty.
14From Ephraim their root they marched
      down into the valley,
   following you, Benjamin, with your kins
      men;
from Machir marched down the
      commanders,
   and from Zebulun those who bear the
      lieutenant's staff;
15the princes of Issachar came with
      Deborah,
   and Issachar faithful to Barak;
   into the valley they rushed at his heels.
Among the clans of Reuben
   there were great searchings of heart.
16Why did you sit still among the
      sheepfolds,
   to hear the whistling for the flocks?
Among the clans of Reuben
   there were great searchings of heart.
17Gilead stayed beyond the Jordan;

and Dan, why did he stay with the
ships?
Asher sat still at the coast of the sea,
staying by his landings
¹⁸Zebulun is a people who risked their
lives to the death;
Naphtali, too, on the heights of the field.
¹⁹"The kings came, they fought;
then fought the kings of Canaan,
at Taanach, by the waters of Megiddo;
they got no spoils of silver.
²⁰From heaven the stars fought,
from their courses they fought against
Sisera.
²¹The torrent Kishon swept them away,
the ancient torrent, the torrent Kishon.
March on, my soul, with might!
²²"Then loud beat the horses' hoofs
with the galloping, galloping of his
steeds.
²³"Curse Meroz, says the angel of the LORD,
curse its inhabitants thoroughly,
because they did not come to the help of
the LORD,
to the help of the LORD against the
mighty.
²⁴"Most blessed of women be Jael,
the wife of Heber the Kenite,
of tent-dwelling women most blessed.
²⁵He asked water and she gave him milk;
she brought him curds in a noble's bowl.

²⁶She sent her hand to the tent peg
and her right hand to the workmen's
mallet;
she struck Sisera;
she crushed his head;
she shattered and pierced his temple.
²⁷Between her feet
he sank, he fell, he lay still;
between her feet
he sank, he fell;
where he sank,
there he fell—dead.
²⁸"Out of the window she peered,
the mother of Sisera wailed through the
lattice:
'Why is his chariot so long in coming?
Why tarry the hoofbeats of his chariots?'
²⁹Her wisest princesses answer,
indeed, she answers herself,
³⁰'Have they not found and divided the
spoil?—
A womb or two for every man;
spoil of dyed materials for Sisera,
spoil of dyed materials embroidered,
two pieces of dyed work embroidered for
the neck as spoil?'
³¹"So may all your enemies perish, O LORD!
But your friends be like the sun as he
rises in his might."
And the land had rest for forty years.

Go Deeper

Singing songs of praise after a miraculous rescue is hardly uncommon in the Bible. Many of the Psalms are praises to God for His provision in dark times. But maybe the most famous of these songs is found in Exodus 15.

Israel had finally been allowed to leave Egypt after years of slavery. But by the time Israel reached the Red Sea, Pharaoh had changed his mind and sent his army after the Hebrew slaves. Trapped between the army of Pharaoh and the Red Sea, the Israelites were about to give up hope.

But God miraculously parted the waters of the Red Sea allowing His

(continued)

Go Deeper Continued . . .

people to cross. The pursuing army didn't get far before the water collapsed, destroying Pharaoh's army. On the far shore, Moses led Israel in a song of praise, "I will sing to the LORD, for he has triumphed gloriously" (Ex. 15:1).

The song ends with a statement as true then as it is today: "The LORD will reign forever and ever" (15:18). Are you trying to fight your own battles today? Why not let the Lord reign in your life?

C hapter 5 in Judges is like the eye of a hurricane. Chronologically, this is about the halfway point in the 300 years of history covered in the book of Judges, and it's one of the brightest spots in this time period. Surrounding it on either side are stories of the deadly cycle of sin, repentance and salvation Israel had fallen into. But here, for one chapter, all is quiet and calm, and the attention is focused where it should be—on God.

Deborah and Barak had just emerged from a miraculous victory against Sisera and his Canaanite army. Remember, Sisera's army possessed 900 iron chariots, cutting-edge military weaponry at that time. An army with iron chariots was considered nearly invincible, and we've already seen that the people of Judah balked once at facing such an army.

Although we don't know how large the rest of Sisera's army was, typically the charioteers would have made up only a small portion. At the very least, number-wise, the two armies were evenly matched. But even with equal numbers, the iron chariots would tip the odds distinctly in favor of Sisera.

But it's not about numbers; it's about trusting God, something both Deborah and Barak exercised. So with his 10,000 men—and God on his side—Barak attacked. The result was a complete rout. Sisera ran away on foot and was killed in his sleep by a woman named Jael.

And with this incredible victory, the cycle breaks for a chapter. We've reached the eye of the storm. We hear the song of Deborah.

How easy it would have been for Deborah to stand up before the people of Israel and graciously accept their praise and honor! Can you see her standing there smiling warmly, waving every now and then, maybe even raising her arm to acknowledge Barak and Jael standing next to her, and all three bowing together?

But that's not what happened. Instead of claiming credit for the victory, Deborah turned her attention, and the attention of Israel, to the Lord God who alone brought them victory. "Hear, O kings; give ear, O princes; to the LORD I will sing" (Judg. 5:3).

Deborah reminded the people of the power of God. "The mountains quaked before the LORD, even Sinai before the LORD, the God of Israel" (5:5). In a land that had for so long been following after the powerless false gods of Canaan, Israel needed to be reminded of the one true God.

In her song, Deborah reminded Israel where their sin had taken them: "The highways were abandoned. . . . When new gods were chosen, then war was in the gates. Was shield or spear to be seen in Israel?" (vv. 6, 8). They were living a life of fear.

Centuries later, Paul would put it this way in his letter to the Romans: "For you did not receive the spirit of slavery to fall back into fear, but you have received the Spirit of adoption as sons, by whom we cry, 'Abba! Father!'" (Rom. 8:15). In a right relationship with God, there is no reason to fear anything because God looks after us like a father looks after his children. Israel had forgotten this important fact.

While it is possible for God to carry out His plan on His own, He has always chosen to use people like you and me to do His work in this world. It's true today, and it was true the day Barak's and Sisera's armies clashed.

In the next portion of her song, Deborah praised God for the people who willingly volunteered for what looked like a suicide mission. Ten thousand men responded to the call of Barak. Ten thousand were willing to fight for God. In contrast to these volun-

> *"Instead of claiming credit for the victory, Deborah turned her attention, and the attention of Israel, to the Lord God who alone brought them victory."*

teers, Deborah had a few words for the tribes, including Reuben and Dan, who instead of rising to the call, stayed home and made excuses.

Today, we're in a battle too. And as Paul reminds us, "we do not wrestle against flesh and blood, but against the rulers, against the authorities, against the cosmic powers over this present darkness, against the spiritual forces of evil in the heavenly places" (Eph. 6:12). But though the fight is different, the fighters are just as important. And God still promises us victory.

It's hard to say how this will look in your own life. But today, make the decision that when the time comes you will go boldly in God's name.

Express It

Sometimes our praise of God is fueled by events in our lives, but the truth is, He is always worthy to be praised. Maybe praise comes easy for you today because of the way God's provided for you. Don't hold back. But even if you're experiencing a difficult time right now, take a few minutes to praise God. Praise Him that He's in control, and praise Him for His servants who willingly give their time for Him.

Consider It

As you read Judges 5:1–31, consider these questions:

1) **What picture of God do you get from the first five verses?**

2) **Why did some of the tribes of Israel participate in the fight while others stayed behind?**

3) **Why is it difficult to volunteer for things?**

4) **Why might Deborah have dwelt on the scene of Sisera's death in her song?**

5) **What spiritual enemies in your life do you need to deal with?**

6) **What are some ways you can praise God for His provision in tough times?**

Gideon—
Learning to Trust

When we first meet Gideon, he is threshing grain—but in hiding. Not long after that, however, Gideon is leading the charge against the Midianites. What caused this dramatic transformation? In this lesson, we'll examine the reason, as well as how we can discover God's will for our lives and why we should avoid putting God to the test.

Judges 6:1–40

Midian Oppresses Israel

6 The people of Israel did what was evil in the sight of the Lord, and the Lord gave them into the hand of Midian seven years. ²And the hand of Midian overpowered Israel, and because of Midian the people of Israel made for themselves the dens that are in the mountains and the caves and the strongholds. ³For whenever the Israelites planted crops, the Midianites and the Amalekites and the people of the East would come up against them. ⁴They would encamp against them and devour the produce of the land, as far as Gaza, and leave no sustenance in Israel and no sheep or ox or donkey. ⁵For they would come up with their livestock and their tents; they would come like locusts in number—both they and their camels could not be counted—so that they laid waste the land as they came in. ⁶And Israel was brought very low because of Midian. And the people of Israel cried out for help to the Lord.

⁷When the people of Israel cried out to the Lord on account of the Midianites, ⁸the Lord sent a prophet to the people of Israel. And he said to them, "Thus says the Lord, the God of Israel: I led you up from Egypt and brought you out of the house of bondage. ⁹And I delivered you from the hand of the Egyptians and from the hand of all who oppressed you, and drove them out before you and gave you their land. ¹⁰And I said to you, 'I am the Lord your God; you shall not fear the gods of the Amorites in whose land you dwell.' But you have not obeyed my voice."

The Call of Gideon

¹¹Now the angel of the Lord came and sat under the terebinth at Ophrah, which belonged to Joash the Abiezrite, while his son Gideon was beating out wheat in the winepress to hide it from the Midianites.

¹²And the angel of the Lord appeared to him and said to him, "The Lord is with you, O mighty man of valor." ¹³And Gideon said to him, "Please, sir, if the Lord is with us, why then has all this happened to us? And where are all his wonderful deeds that our fathers recounted to us, saying, 'Did not the Lord bring us up from Egypt?' But now the Lord has forsaken us and given us into the hand of Midian." ¹⁴And the Lord turned to him and said, "Go in this might of yours and save Israel from the hand of Midian; do not I send you?" ¹⁵And he said to him, "Please, Lord, how can I save Israel? Behold, my clan is the weakest in Manasseh, and I am the least in my father's house." ¹⁶And the Lord said to him, "But I will be with you, and you shall strike the Midian-

Key Verse

And the Lord *said to him,* "But I *will be with you, and you shall strike the Midianites as one man"* (Judg. 6:16).

ites as one man." ¹⁷And he said to him, "If now I have found favor in your eyes, then show me a sign that it is you who speaks with me. ¹⁸Please do not depart from here until I come to you and bring out my present and set it before you." And he said, "I will stay till you return."

¹⁹So Gideon went into his house and prepared a young goat and unleavened cakes from an ephah of flour. The meat he put in a basket, and the broth he put in a pot, and brought them to him under the

terebinth and presented them. ²⁰And the angel of God said to him, "Take the meat and the unleavened cakes, and put them on this rock, and pour the broth over them." And he did so. ²¹Then the angel of the Lord reached out the tip of the staff that was in his hand and touched the meat and the unleavened cakes. And fire sprang up from the rock and consumed the flesh and the unleavened cakes. And the angel of the Lord vanished from his sight. ²²Then Gideon perceived that he was the angel of the Lord. And Gideon said, "Alas, O Lord God! For now I have seen the angel of the Lord face to face." ²³But the Lord said to him, "Peace be to you. Do not fear; you shall not die." ²⁴Then Gideon built an altar there to the Lord and called it, The Lord is Peace. To this day it still stands at Ophrah, which belongs to the Abiezrites.

²⁵That night the Lord said to him, "Take your father's bull, and the second bull seven years old, and pull down the altar of Baal that your father has, and cut down the Asherah that is beside it ²⁶and build an altar to the Lord your God on the top of the stronghold here, with stones laid in due order. Then take the second bull and offer it as a burnt offering with the wood of the Asherah that you shall cut down." ²⁷So Gideon took ten men of his servants and did as the Lord had told him. But because he was too afraid of his family and the men of the town to do it by day, he did it by night.

Gideon Destroys the Altar of Baal

²⁸When the men of the town rose early in the morning, behold, the altar of Baal was broken down, and the Asherah beside it was cut down, and the second bull was offered on the altar that had been built. ²⁹And they said to one another, "Who has done this thing?" And after they had searched and inquired, they said, "Gideon the son of Joash has done this thing." ³⁰Then the men of the town said to Joash,

"Bring out your son, that he may die, for he has broken down the altar of Baal and cut down the Asherah beside it." ³¹But Joash said to all who stood against him, "Will you contend for Baal? Or will you save him? Whoever contends for him shall be put to death by morning. If he is a god, let him contend for himself, because his altar has been broken down." ³²Therefore on that day Gideon was called Jerubbaal, that is to say, "Let Baal contend against him," because he broke down his altar.

³³Now all the Midianites and the Amalekites and the people of the East came together, and they crossed the Jordan and encamped in the Valley of Jezreel. ³⁴But the Spirit of the Lord clothed Gideon, and he sounded the trumpet, and the Abiezrites were called out to follow him. ³⁵And he sent messengers throughout all Manasseh, and they too were called out to follow him. And he sent messengers to Asher, Zebulun, and Naphtali, and they went up to meet them.

The Sign of the Fleece

³⁶Then Gideon said to God, "If you will save Israel by my hand, as you have said, ³⁷behold, I am laying a fleece of wool on the threshing floor. If there is dew on the fleece alone, and it is dry on all the ground, then I shall know that you will save Israel by my hand, as you have said." ³⁸And it was so. When he rose early next morning and squeezed the fleece, he wrung enough dew from the fleece to fill a bowl with water. ³⁹Then Gideon said to God, "Let not your anger burn against me; let me speak just once more. Please let me test just once more with the fleece. Please let it be dry on the fleece only, and on all the ground let there be dew." ⁴⁰And God did so that night; and it was dry on the fleece only, and on all the ground there was dew.

Go Deeper

Gideon wasn't the first person to wonder if he was following God's will, and he definitely won't be the last. Believers of all centuries have asked how we can know God's will.

In the Old Testament, the priests would use the Urim and Thummim to discern God's will. Not much is known about what the Urim and Thummim actually were. But based on passages like Exodus 28:30 and Numbers 27:21, it seems they were objects kept in the breastpiece of the priest. They were God's ordained way of discerning His will.

Today in New Testament times, things are different. As the apostle Peter reminds us, we as Christ-followers are being made into a new kind of priesthood (1 Pet. 2:9). But, even though we haven't been given the Urim and Thummim, we've been given something just as effective in determining the will of God in our lives—the Holy Spirit.

Jesus reassured His disciples that after He returned to heaven, God would send "another Helper, to be with you forever" (John 14:16). This Helper, the Holy Spirit, will "teach you all things and bring to your remembrance all that I [Jesus] have said to you" (14:26).

Are you spending time with God? If not, don't be surprised if His will is hard to discern. But if you are concerned about following God's path through life, take time to read His Word and spend time in prayer. The more time you spend with Him, the easier it will be to hear Him when He calls.

With the start of Gideon's story, we enter the last half of the time of the judges. After the 40 years of peace that came from Deborah and Barak's defeat of Sisera, a new enemy arose.

This time it's the Midianites who oppress Israel, but the reason is still the same: "The people of Israel did what was evil in the sight of the LORD" (Judg. 6:1). The Israelites worshiped new gods made of wood and stone, and they followed the customs of their pagan neighbors.

The Midianites were a brutal army who exercised hit-and-run tactics. During every harvest, Midian would sweep in and take all the produce and grain. Because of their camels, they were able to travel long distances swiftly and attack quickly. In the days of

Shamgar, people stayed off the roads; in the days of Gideon, they hid in caves.

When God called up the Midianites, it's almost as if He was directly challenging the false gods of Israel to defend them. In fact, Gideon's first task was to prove this by "pull[ing] down the altar of Baal that your father has, and cut down the Asherah that is beside it and build an altar to the LORD your God on the top of the stronghold here" (Judg. 6:25–26).

Gideon obeyed, and Baal didn't respond. But while the people cried out for Gideon to be put to death, Gideon's father stood up and basically said, "If Baal is truly a god, let him deal with Gideon" (6:31).

Through this experience, the weakness of this false god was proven, and Gideon was reassured that he was the man to drive out the armies of Midian. So, Gideon sent messengers throughout Israel, and 32,000 men responded to the call. But even with such an army around him, Gideon faltered in his trust of God's leading.

When people look at verses 36–40 and see Gideon laying out the fleeces, they often see it as an acceptable way of determining God's will for their life. We say things like, "God, if you want me to lose weight, please close the donut shop on my way to work," or "If you really want me to have that new couch, please put it on sale for $200." That's laying out a fleece, using some test to discover God's will. But that's not the right way to approach God!

In Gideon's case, God had already told Gideon that he would win, and Gideon knew this: "If you will save Israel by my hand, as you have said . . ." (Judg. 6:36). A lot of the times when we "lay out the fleece," God has already explicitly spelled out His will in the Bible for particular areas of our lives.

In addition, laying out fleeces is a sign of a person's doubt. Did you notice that "if" in Gideon's statement? Even though God had reaffirmed Gideon's calling several times, Gideon somehow was able to say "if." But God has always promised to guide us. The Bible is filled with promises for those who make the Lord their guide. It's not down a path of "if's," but a path of certainty.

> *" The real way to know God's will for your life is not through silly tests that don't prove anything. We find God's will by listening to His guidance. "*

On top of that, even when God did grant Gideon's first request, Gideon asked for another sign. The first sign wasn't enough for him. When you dictate to God that He has only two ways of revealing His will, you open yourself up to more doubts and uncertainty. What if on Gideon's second test, the ground was wet only up to one foot away from the fleece? Would that have been far enough? What if a single drop of dew appeared on the fleece? It's still *mostly* dry. God was gracious in responding to Gideon's requests, but the laying out of fleeces didn't tell Gideon anything he didn't already know.

The real way to know God's will for your life is not through silly tests that don't prove anything. We find God's will by listening to His guidance. For that we have the Bible, the very words of God. And as a Christian, you have the Counselor, the Holy Spirit Himself, guiding you along the road God has marked for you. Instead of laying out fleeces, listen for God's advice from His Word.

Express It

One of the biggest obstacles to being used by God is fear and doubt. But God is a gracious God. If you're unsure about where He's calling you, ask Him to calm your fears and reassure your doubts. If on the other hand you know where God is calling but are afraid of the consequences, ask God for the courage to go boldly in His name. And remember to praise Him for the results.

Consider It

As you read Judges 6:1–40, consider these questions:

1) Based on verses 3–6, how did Midian oppress Israel?

_____

_____

2) In verse 7, how does God respond to Israel's call for help?

_____

_____

3) Where do we first meet Gideon? Does he seem a logical choice for a future judge?

_____

_____

_____

4) What assurances does the angel of the Lord give Gideon of his calling?

_____

_____

_____

5) What is Gideon's response when he recognizes his visitor?

_____

_____

_____

6) What is the significance of the name Jerubbaal?

_____

_____

_____

7) What evidence is there that Gideon was acting out of doubt and fear when he laid out the fleeces?

_____

_____

_____

8) What do we learn about God in His response to Gideon about the fleeces?

_____

_____

_____

Gideon— Finishing Well

Sometimes our greatest victories can lead to our most shameful defeats. After leading God's army against the Midianites and winning a miraculous victory, Gideon's pride starts the nation on the downward spiral—again. In this lesson, we'll look at Gideon's mistakes and learn how to avoid them.

Judges 7:1–8:35

Gideon's Three Hundred Men

7 Then Jerubbaal (that is, Gideon) and all the people who were with him rose early and encamped beside the spring of Harod. And the camp of Midian was north of them, by the hill of Moreh, in the valley.

²The Lord said to Gideon, "The people with you are too many for me to give the Midianites into their hand, lest Israel boast over me, saying, 'My own hand has saved me.' ³Now therefore proclaim in the ears of the people, saying, 'Whoever is fearful and trembling, let him return home and hurry away from Mount Gilead.'" Then he went 22,000 of the people returned, and 10,000 remained.

⁴And the Lord said to Gideon, "The people are still too many. Take them down to the water, and I will test them for you there, and anyone of whom I say to you, 'This one shall go with you,' shall go with you, and anyone of whom I say to you, 'This one shall not go with you,' shall not go." ⁵So he brought the people down to the water. And the Lord said to Gideon, "Every one who laps the water with his tongue, as a dog laps, you shall set by himself. Likewise, every one who kneels down to drink." ⁶And the number of those who lapped, putting their hands to their mouths, was 300 men, but all the rest of the people knelt down to drink water. ⁷And the Lord said to Gideon, "With the 300 men who lapped I will save you and give the Midianites into your hand, and let all the others go every man to his home." ⁸So the people took provisions in their hands, and their trumpets. And he sent all the rest of Israel every man to his tent, but retained the 300 men. And the camp of Midian was below him in the valley.

⁹That same night the Lord said to him, "Arise, go down against the camp, for I have given it into your hand. ¹⁰But if you are afraid to go down, go down to the camp with Purah your servant. ¹¹And you shall hear what they say, and afterward your hands shall be strengthened to go down against the camp." Then he went down with Purah his servant to the outposts of the armed men who were in the camp. ¹²And the Midianites and the Amalekites and all the people of the East lay along the valley like locusts in abundance, and their camels were without number, as the sand that is on the seashore in abundance. ¹³When Gideon came, behold, a man was telling a dream to his comrade. And he said, "Behold, I dreamed a dream, and behold, a cake of barley bread tumbled into the camp of Midian and came to the tent and struck it so that it fell and turned it upside down, so that the tent lay flat." ¹⁴And his comrade answered, "This is no other than the sword of Gideon the son of Joash, a man of Israel; God has given into his hand Midian and all the camp."

¹⁵As soon as Gideon heard the telling of the dream and its interpretation, he worshiped. And he returned to the camp of Israel and said, "Arise, for the Lord has given the host of Midian into your hand." ¹⁶And he divided the 300 men into three companies and put trumpets into the hands of all of them and empty jars, with torches inside the jars. ¹⁷And he said to them, "Look at me, and do likewise. When I come to the outskirts of the camp, do as I do. ¹⁸When I blow the trumpet, I and all who are with me, then blow the trumpets also on every side of all the camp and shout, 'For the Lord and for Gideon.'"

Gideon Defeats Midian

¹⁹So Gideon and the hundred men who were with him came to the outskirts of the camp at the beginning of the middle watch, when they had just set the watch.

And they blew the trumpets and smashed the jars that were in their hands. ²⁰Then the three companies blew the trumpets and broke the jars. They held in their left hands the torches, and in their right hands the trumpets to blow. And they cried out, "A sword for the Lord and for Gideon!" ²¹Every man stood in his place around the camp, and all the army ran. They cried out and fled. ²²When they blew the 300 trumpets, the Lord set every man's sword against his comrade and against all the army. And the army fled as far as Beth-shittah toward Zererah, as far as the border of Abel-meholah, by Tabbath. ²³And the men of Israel were called out from Naphtali and from Asher and from all Manasseh, and they pursued after Midian.

²⁴Gideon sent messengers throughout all the hill country of Ephraim, saying, "Come down against the Midianites and capture the waters against them, as far as Beth-barah, and also the Jordan." So all the men of Ephraim were called out, and they captured the waters as far as Beth-barah, and also the Jordan. ²⁵And they captured the two princes of Midian, Oreb and Zeeb. They killed Oreb at the rock of Oreb, and Zeeb they killed at the winepress of Zeeb. Then they pursued Midian, and they brought the heads of Oreb and Zeeb to Gideon across the Jordan.

Gideon Defeats Zebah and Zalmunna

8 Then the men of Ephraim said to him, "What is this that you have done to us, not to call us when you went to fight with Midian?" And they accused him fiercely. ²And he said to them, "What have I done now in comparison with you? Is not the gleaning of the grapes of Ephraim better than the grape harvest of Abiezer? ³God has given into your hands the princes of Midian, Oreb and Zeeb. What have I been able to do in comparison with you?" Then their anger against him subsided when he said this.

⁴And Gideon came to the Jordan and crossed over, he and the 300 men who were with him, exhausted yet pursuing. ⁵So he said to the men of Succoth, "Please give loaves of bread to the people who follow me, for they are exhausted, and I am pursuing after Zebah and Zalmunna, the kings of Midian." ⁶And the officials of Succoth said, "Are the hands of Zebah and Zalmunna already in your hand, that we should give bread to your army?" ⁷So Gideon said, "Well then, when the Lord has given Zebah and Zalmunna into my hand, I will flail your flesh with the thorns of the wilderness and with briers." ⁸And from there he went up to Penuel, and spoke to them in the same way, and the men of Penuel answered him as the men of Succoth had answered. ⁹And he said to the men of Penuel, "When I come again in peace, I will break down this tower."

¹⁰Now Zebah and Zalmunna were in Karkor with their army, about 15,000 men, all who were left of all the army of the people of the East, for there had fallen 120,000 men who drew the sword. ¹¹And Gideon went up by the way of the tent dwellers east of Nobah and Jogbehah and attacked the army, for the army felt secure. ¹²And Zebah and Zalmunna fled, and he pursued them and captured the two kings of Midian, Zebah and Zalmunna, and he threw all the army into a panic.

¹³Then Gideon the son of Joash returned from the battle by the ascent of Heres. ¹⁴And he captured a young man of Succoth and questioned him. And he wrote down for him the officials and elders of Succoth, seventy-seven men. ¹⁵And he came to the men of Succoth and said, "Behold Zebah and Zalmunna, about whom you taunted me, saying, 'Are the hands of Zebah and Zalmunna already in your hand, that we should give bread to your men who are exhausted?'" ¹⁶And he took the elders of the city, and he took thorns of the wilderness and briers and with them taught the men

of Succoth a lesson. [17]And he broke down the tower of Penuel and killed the men of the city.

[18]Then he said to Zebah and Zalmunna, "Where are the men whom you killed at Tabor?" They answered, "As you are, so were they. Every one of them resembled the son of a king." [19]And he said, "They were my brothers, the sons of my mother. As the LORD lives, if you had saved them alive, I would not kill you." [20]So he said to Jether his firstborn, "Rise and kill them!" But the young man did not draw his sword, for he was afraid, because he was still a young man. [21]Then Zebah and Zalmunna said, "Rise yourself and fall upon us, for as the man is, so is his strength." And Gideon arose and killed Zebah and Zalmunna, and he took the crescent ornaments that were on the necks of their camels.

Gideon's Ephod

[22]Then the men of Israel said to Gideon, "Rule over us, you and your son and your grandson also, for you have saved us from the hand of Midian." [23]Gideon said to them, "I will not rule over you, and my son will not rule over you; the LORD will rule over you." [24]And Gideon said to them, "Let me make a request of you: every one of you give me the earrings from his spoil." (For they had golden earrings, because they were Ishmaelites.) [25]And they answered, "We will willingly give them." And they spread a cloak, and every man threw in it the earrings of his spoil. [26]And the weight of the golden earrings that he requested was 1,700 shekels of gold, besides the crescent ornaments and the pendants and the purple garments worn by the kings of Midian, and besides the collars that were around the necks of their camels. [27]And Gideon made an ephod of it and put it in his city, in Ophrah. And all Israel whored after it there, and it became a snare to Gideon and to his family. [28]So Midian was subdued before the people of Israel, and they raised their heads no more. And the land had rest forty years in the days of Gideon.

> # Key Verse
>
> *And Gideon made an ephod . . . and it became a snare to Gideon and to his family* (Judg. 8:27).

The Death of Gideon

[29]Jerubbaal the son of Joash went and lived in his own house. [30]Now Gideon had seventy sons, his own offspring, for he had many wives. [31]And his concubine who was in Shechem also bore him a son, and he called his name Abimelech. [32]And Gideon the son of Joash died in a good old age and was buried in the tomb of Joash his father, at Ophrah of the Abiezrites.

[33]As soon as Gideon died, the people of Israel turned again and whored after the Baals and made Baal-berith their god. [34]And the people of Israel did not remember the LORD their God, who had delivered them from the hand of all their enemies on every side, [35]and they did not show steadfast love to the family of Jerubbaal (that is, Gideon) in return for all the good that he had done to Israel.

Go Deeper

When you look closely at the description of Gideon's battle against the Midianites, it's clear that in that initial encounter, the Israelites didn't raise a sword. "The LORD set every man's sword against his comrade and against all the army" (Judg. 7:22).

This brings us to a very important point when it comes to spiritual warfare. It's not you or I who fight against the devil; it's God.

Someday God is going to deal with Satan once and for all. In the meantime, we've been given the equipment we need to withstand the attacks of the evil one. In Ephesians 6, the apostle Paul uses the metaphor of a warrior dressing for battle to describe our spiritual armor.

We cloth ourselves with truth, righteousness, faith, readiness, salvation and the Word of God. When we immerse ourselves in living a godly lifestyle, we can be confident that we'll withstand any attack the devil throws at us.

I f Gideon's story ended after chapter 7, we'd have an incredible picture of how God can transform a person's life from one of defeat to one of victory. In the first two chapters that tell Gideon's story, we see his journey from a man threshing grain in hiding to leading an army against the Midianites.

God reassured Gideon of his calling by appearing to him and then graciously obliging Gideon's request for proof of God's will. God followed this by commanding Gideon to clean up his home by destroying the altar to Baal kept by his father. This not only sent a clear statement that God will not have His glory shared by false gods, it also demonstrated the utter powerlessness of these so-called gods.

In fact, the whole structure of Gideon's battle was designed to demonstrate God's power. When Gideon first assembled his army, he had 32,000 men to go up against the 135,000 of Midian. A long shot to be sure. Soon the army was reduced to 10,000 men and again to 300. That's 450 Midianites for every Israelite.

God gave His reason for this drastic reduction in force when He told Gideon, "lest Israel boast over me, saying 'My own hand has saved me'" (Judg. 7:2). God wanted there to be no doubt that when Israel beat the Midianites, it was God's doing and not the work of men.

Chapter 7 ends with the miraculous defeat of the Midianite army. Gideon learned to trust God in the most extreme of circumstances and found victorious living in a life plagued by defeats. Today, this is still the best way to a truly victorious life. The apostle Paul tells us to give God our fears and worries, "and the peace of God, which surpasses all understanding, will guard your hearts and your minds in Christ Jesus" (Phil. 4:7)

Unfortunately, this isn't the end of Gideon's story. Gideon learned that complete trust in God leads to incredible victories in His name. But he's also about to learn that times of victory are when Satan presses his attack all the harder.

With the Midianites and their princes killed, Gideon returned home a hero. "Then the men of Israel said to Gideon, 'Rule over us, you and your son and your grandson also, for you have saved us from the hand of Midian'" (Judg. 8:22). They missed the point. There's not one mention of God at all in their request. They've already forgotten that only God could lead an army outnumbered 450 to 1 to victory. They forgot crying out to God for help. Instead of worshiping God, the Israelites wanted to make Gideon their king and give him credit for the victory.

When God uses us, He doesn't lead us to a place of self-reliance, as the Israelites supposed. He doesn't lead us to say, "I had it in me all along!" When God uses us, He brings us to a place of "God-reliance," a place where we declare for the world to hear *soli deo gloria*, "Glory to God alone!"

Gideon flatly refused the request saying, "The LORD will rule over you" (v. 23). But here he faltered. Gideon asked the people to make him an ephod—a garment worn by priests. Evidently Gideon wanted to restore to Israel a symbol of the priesthood. But it didn't work out like that. Instead, the ephod became another idol to the Israelites. They worshiped the ephod instead of the living God.

> **" Our times of greatest victory are often followed by our times of greatest temptation. "**

Gideon had done the right thing by reminding Israel that God is their King, but he had no business creating a priestly garment. God appointed the tribe of Levi to fill the priestly role in Israel. This may not seem like a big mistake, especially considering that Gideon was acting on good intentions. But good intentions become evil when not built on God's will.

Even though he refused the kingship, it appears that Gideon allowed himself the benefits of a king, evidenced by his many wives and 70 sons. In fact, he named one of his children Abimelech, or "my father is king."

Our times of greatest victory are often followed by our times of greatest temptation. In victory, it's easy to want to claim just a little credit for ourselves. Though Gideon refused a lot, he made some small concessions that ultimately launched Israel into some of its darkest days. In our days of victory, let's remember to keep our eyes on God and God alone.

Express It

It seems like a Catch-22—the more we rely on God and give Him control of our lives, the more we are attacked and tempted away from Him. But when you are feeling threatened and tempted by Satan, take that as your cue to call on God. Ask for His help in meeting the enemy. Praise God that He's changing you into the person He made you to be—the devil doesn't attack spiritual wash-outs.

Consider It

As you read Judges 7:1–8:35, consider these questions:

1) Have there been times in your life when you worried about how God would pull you through?

2) How did you respond in those situations?

3) How does God reassure Gideon that the Midianites will be defeated?

4) What was the Ephraimites' argument against Gideon?

5) How did Gideon respond to their complaints?

6) What are our "idols" today? What things pull our attention away from God?

7) What do these things promise? Or, what do they threaten will happen if you don't pursue them?

8) How would God respond to that?

Lesson
9

Abimelech— Grasping for Power

Abimelech's story is filled with violence and bloodshed as he seeks to wrest control of Israel for himself. Through this lesson, we'll see the danger of grasping for power outside of God's will and the importance of instilling godly values in our children.

Judges 9:1–56

Abimelech's Conspiracy

9 Now Abimelech the son of Jerubbaal went to Shechem to his mother's relatives and said to them and to the whole clan of his mother's family, ²"Say in the ears of all the leaders of Shechem, 'Which is better for you, that all seventy of the sons of Jerubbaal rule over you, or that one rule over you?' Remember also that I am your bone and your flesh."

³And his mother's relatives spoke all these words on his behalf in the ears of all the leaders of Shechem, and their hearts inclined to follow Abimelech, for they said, "He is our brother." ⁴And they gave him seventy pieces of silver out of the house of Baal-berith with which Abimelech hired worthless and reckless fellows, who followed him. ⁵And he went to his father's house at Ophrah and killed his brothers the sons of Jerubbaal, seventy men, on one stone. But Jotham the youngest son of Jerubbaal was left, for he hid himself. ⁶And all the leaders of Shechem came together, and all Beth-millo, and they went and made Abimelech king, by the oak of the pillar at Shechem.

⁷When it was told to Jotham, he went and stood on top of Mount Gerizim and cried aloud and said to them, "Listen to me, you leaders of Shechem, that God may listen to you. ⁸The trees once went out to anoint a king over them, and they said to the olive tree, 'Reign over us.' ⁹But the olive tree said to them, 'Shall I leave my abundance, by which gods and men are honored, and go hold sway over the trees?' ¹⁰And the trees said to the fig tree, 'You come and reign over us.' ¹¹But the fig tree said to them, 'Shall I leave my sweetness and my good fruit and go hold sway over the trees?' ¹²And the trees said to the vine, 'You come and reign over us.' ¹³But the vine said to them, 'Shall I leave my wine that cheers God and men and go hold sway over the trees?' ¹⁴Then all the trees said to the bramble, 'You come and reign over us.' ¹⁵And the bramble said to the trees, 'If in good faith you are anointing me king over you, then come and take refuge in my shade, but if not, let fire come out of the bramble and devour the cedars of Lebanon.'

¹⁶"Now therefore, if you acted in good faith and integrity when you made Abimelech king, and if you have dealt well with Jerubbaal and his house and have done to him as his deeds deserved— ¹⁷for my father fought for you and risked his life and delivered you from the hand of Midian, ¹⁸and you have risen up against my father's house this day and have killed his sons, seventy men on one stone, and have made Abimelech, the son of his female servant, king over the leaders of Shechem, because he is your relative— ¹⁹if you then have acted in good faith and integrity with Jerubbaal and with his house this day, then rejoice in Abimelech, and let him also rejoice in you. ²⁰But if not, let fire come out from Abimelech and devour the leaders of Shechem and Beth-millo; and let fire come out from the leaders of Shechem and from Beth-millo and devour Abimelech." ²¹And Jotham ran away and fled and went to Beer and lived there, because of Abimelech his brother.

The Downfall of Abimelech

²²Abimelech ruled over Israel three years. ²³And God sent an evil spirit between Abimelech and the leaders of Shechem, and the leaders of Shechem dealt treacherously with Abimelech, ²⁴that the violence done to the seventy sons of Jerubbaal might come, and their blood be laid on Abimelech their brother, who killed them, and on the men of Shechem, who

strengthened his hands to kill his brothers. [25]And the leaders of Shechem put men in ambush against him on the mountaintops, and they robbed all who passed by them along that way. And it was told to Abimelech.

[26]And Gaal the son of Ebed moved into Shechem with his relatives, and the leaders of Shechem put confidence in him. [27]And they went out into the field and gathered the grapes from their vineyards and trod them and held a festival; and they went into the house of their god and ate and drank and reviled Abimelech. [28]And Gaal the son of Ebed said, "Who is Abimelech, and who are we of Shechem, that we should serve him? Is he not the son of Jerubbaal, and is not Zebul his officer? Serve the men of Hamor the father of Shechem; but why should we serve him? [29]Would that this people were under my hand! Then I would remove Abimelech. I would say to Abimelech, 'Increase your army, and come out.'"

[30]When Zebul the ruler of the city heard the words of Gaal the son of Ebed, his anger was kindled. [31]And he sent messengers to Abimelech secretly, saying, "Behold, Gaal the son of Ebed and his relatives have come to Shechem, and they are stirring up the city against you. [32]Now therefore, go by night, you and the people who are with you, and set an ambush in the field. [33]Then in the morning, as soon as the sun is up, rise early and rush upon the city. And when he and the people who are with him come out against you, you may do to them as your hand finds to do."

[34]So Abimelech and all the men who were with him rose up by night and set an ambush against Shechem in four companies. [35]And Gaal the son of Ebed went out and stood in the entrance of the gate of the city, and Abimelech and the people who were with him rose from the ambush. [36]And when Gaal saw the people, he said to Zebul, "Look, people are coming down from the mountaintops!" And Zebul said to him, "You mistake the shadow of the mountains for men." [37]Gaal spoke again and said, "Look, people are coming down from the center of the land, and one company is coming from the direction of the Diviners' Oak." [38]Then Zebul said to him, "Where is your mouth now, you who said, 'Who is Abimelech, that we should serve him?' Are not these the people whom you despised? Go out now and fight with them." [39]And Gaal went out at the head of the leaders of Shechem and fought with Abimelech. [40]And Abimelech chased him, and he fled before him. And many fell wounded, up to the entrance of the gate. [41]And Abimelech lived at Arumah, and Zebul drove out Gaal and his relatives, so that they could not dwell at Shechem.

[42]On the following day, the people went out into the field, and Abimelech was told. [43]He took his people and divided them into three companies and set an ambush in the fields. And he looked and saw the people coming out of the city. So he rose against them and killed them. [44]Abimelech and the company that was with him rushed forward and stood at the entrance of the gate of the city, while the two companies rushed upon all who were in the field and killed them. [45]And Abimelech fought against the city all that day. He captured the city and killed the people who were in it, and he razed the city and sowed it with salt.

[46]When all the leaders of the Tower of Shechem heard of it, they entered the stronghold of the house of El-berith. [47]Abimelech was told that all the leaders of the Tower of Shechem were gathered together. [48]And Abimelech went up to Mount Zalmon, he and all the people who were with him. And Abimelech took an axe in his hand and cut down a bundle of brushwood and took it up and laid it on his shoulder. And he said to the men who

were with him, "What you have seen me do, hurry and do as I have done." ⁴⁹So every one of the people cut down his bundle and following Abimelech put it against the stronghold, and they set the stronghold on fire over them, so that all the people of the Tower of Shechem also died, about 1,000 men and women.

⁵⁰Then Abimelech went to Thebez and encamped against Thebez and captured it. ⁵¹But there was a strong tower within the city, and all the men and women and all the leaders of the city fled to it and shut themselves in, and they went up to the roof of the tower. ⁵²And Abimelech came to the tower and fought against it and drew near to the door of the tower to burn it with fire. ⁵³And a certain woman threw an upper millstone on Abimelech's head and crushed his skull. ⁵⁴Then he called quickly to the young man his armor-bearer and said to him, "Draw your sword and kill me,

lest they say of me, 'A woman killed him.'" And his young man thrust him through, and he died. ⁵⁵And when the men of Israel saw that Abimelech was dead, everyone departed to his home. ⁵⁶Thus God returned the evil of Abimelech, which he committed against his father in killing his seventy brothers.

Key Verse

Thus God returned the evil of Abimelech, which he committed against his father in killing his seventy brothers (Judg. 9:56).

Go Deeper

Jotham might have been the first to compare the servants of God with trees. But he wasn't the last. One of the best loved Psalms uses this same comparison to describe the one who walks with the Lord.

Psalm 1:3 says that the one who walks with God "is like a tree planted by streams of water that yields its fruit in its season, and its leaf does not wither. In all that he does, he prospers."

The psalmist contrasts this with those who walk in evil, who are described as

having no place in the company of the righteous. All they do leads to destruction. How true this was of Abimelech who took his own path and died a shameful death!

It would be enough for God to command our obedience. He is the Creator God and intrinsically worthy of all glory and honor whether we want to give it or not. But it's a sign of God's love and grace that He allows us to feel joy and fulfillment when we lift Him up. It is literally what we are created for.

Chapter 9 of Judges is a rather tragic footnote in an already tragic portion of Israel's history. This chapter is the story of Abimelech, a son of Gideon.

While victorious at times, Gideon ended his life in compromise and disgrace. Though he recognized God's guidance and lordship after the defeat of Midian, he came to trust in himself. He may have refused the kingship, but he allowed himself all the perks.

Gideon had many wives, and through them he had 70 sons. He also had a concubine in the city of Shechem, with whom he had a son named "Abimelech," which means "my father is king." That name itself is an indication of Gideon's heart.

After Gideon died, the people should have looked to God for their guidance. God reminded them many times of how He helped them in the past (Judg. 2:1; 6:8). Through God's guidance and power, the people of Israel had experienced many miraculous victories. But instead of turning to God, they turned to someone else. And Abimelech took it upon himself to become the next leader in Israel.

To secure the leadership, Abimelech launched a bloody attack against the 70 sons of Gideon, killed all but one of them, and proclaimed himself king of Israel. Though the office of the judges was never hereditary, Israel had almost completely lost sight of who they were. They had become so much like the surrounding nations and adopted their customs and religious practices. Only one son, Jotham, survived the bloody coup, and he appeared at Abimelech's coronation to tell a strange story.

Jotham's story involves a group of trees searching for a new king. Now, the trees weren't without a king; the problem is they wanted a new one. The trees approach an olive tree, a fig tree and a grapevine and get the same answer from each—no.

These three understood that they were functioning as God created them. And while they carried out that purpose, both God and men were pleased with the results. Even though the offer to be king of the trees sounded tempting, it wasn't what God had made them to do.

The same is true in our lives. Many people dream of the perfect job and the perfect home with the perfect family. But if pursuing your dreams takes you away from where God has "planted" you, it's time to stop and reevaluate your motives. The olive tree, fig tree, and grapevine knew this and lived a contented, happy life.

The trees finally turned to a thorn bush with their offer of kingship. Can you imagine? In human terms, this is equivalent to people so desperate for leadership that they turn to a common criminal. How long do you suppose a situation like that might last?

In Abimelech's case, it was three years before Israel had enough of his kingship. But it wasn't just the people who were against Abimelech; God was too. We read in Judges 9:23 that "God sent an evil spirit between Abimelech and the leaders of Shechem." This in itself is the fulfillment of a promise God made many years earlier: "He [God] will not be slack with one who hates him. He will repay him to his face" (Deut. 7:10). Abimelech learned the hard way that anyone who fights against God fights a losing battle.

The story of Abimelech ends with him on a bloodthirsty pursuit of anyone who challenged his authority as king. His "rule," however, suddenly ends when a woman on a tower drops a millstone on his head.

The story of Abimelech shows us the danger of grasping for power beyond what God has given. The story of the trees shows us that the best place to be is right where God has placed us. There, like the olive tree, the fig tree and the grapevine, we'll be able to be a pleasure to both God and men.

Express It

In today's culture where "cutthroat" business tactics are regarded as the only way to get ahead, it may seem counterintuitive to pull back and give God control of your future. If that's the case, ask God to give you a peace about His guidance. Spend time walking in the way of God and delighting in reading His Word. Ask God to give you a hunger for His work.

Consider It

As you read Judges 9:1–56, consider these questions:

1) How does Abimelech get the support of Shechem?

2) How is Abimelech's coup funded?

3) Why did Abimelech think he deserved the kingship?

4) In verse 23, what happens to the relationship between Abimelech and the people of Shechem?

5) How does Abimelech deal with the city of Shechem?

6) How does Abimelech's rule end?

7) What is God's role in this chapter?

8) What does this teach you about God's personality?

How the Mighty Have Fallen

Ever since the death of Joshua, the history of Israel in the book of Judges had been one of compromise and partial obedience, to outright rejection of God and ignorance of His commands. In this lesson, we'll look at the importance of keeping a daily relationship with God and the difference between crying out to God in regret and bowing before Him in repentance.

Judges 10:1–18

Tola and Jair

10 After Abimelech there arose to save Israel Tola the son of Puah, son of Dodo, a man of Issachar, and he lived at Shamir in the hill country of Ephraim. ²And he judged Israel twenty-three years. Then he died and was buried at Shamir.

³After him arose Jair the Gileadite, who judged Israel twenty-two years. ⁴And he had thirty sons who rode on thirty donkeys, and they had thirty cities, called Havvoth-jair to this day, which are in the land of Gilead. ⁵And Jair died and was buried in Kamon.

Further Disobedience and Oppression

⁶The people of Israel again did what was evil in the sight of the LORD and served the Baals and the Ashtaroth, the gods of Syria, the gods of Sidon, the gods of Moab, the gods of the Ammonites, and the gods of the Philistines. And they forsook the LORD and did not serve him. ⁷So the anger of the LORD was kindled against Israel, and he sold them into the hand of the Philistines and into the hand of the Ammonites, ⁸and they crushed and oppressed the people of Israel that year. For eighteen years they oppressed all the people of Israel who were beyond the Jordan in the land of the Amorites, which is in Gilead. ⁹And the Ammonites crossed the Jordan to fight also against Judah and against Benjamin and against the house of Ephraim, so that Israel was severely distressed.

¹⁰And the people of Israel cried out to the LORD, saying, "We have sinned against you, because we have forsaken our God and have served the Baals." ¹¹And the LORD said to the people of Israel, "Did I not save you from the Egyptians and from the Amorites, from the Ammonites and from the Philistines? ¹²The Sidonians also, and the Amalekites and the Maonites oppressed you, and you cried out to me, and I saved you out of their hand. ¹³Yet you have forsaken me and served other gods; therefore I will save you no more. ¹⁴Go and cry out to the gods whom you have chosen; let them save you in the time of your distress." ¹⁵And the people of Israel said to the LORD, "We have sinned; do to us whatever seems good to you. Only please deliver us this day." ¹⁶So they put away the foreign gods from among them and served the LORD, and he became impatient over the misery of Israel.

Key Verse

And the people of Israel cried out to the LORD, saying, "We have sinned against you, because we have forsaken our God and have served the Baals" (Judg. 10:10).

---

¹⁷Then the Ammonites were called to arms, and they encamped in Gilead. And the people of Israel came together, and they encamped at Mizpah. ¹⁸And the people, the leaders of Gilead, said one to another, "Who is the man who will begin to fight against the Ammonites? He shall be head over all the inhabitants of Gilead."

Go Deeper

A word that's often used to describe Israel in the days of the Judges is "syncretism." Basically this means that the religious customs of Israel began to get mixed up and combined with the religious customs of the Canaanites they lived around. In the Book of Judges, we see many times the danger of syncretism.

Adopting the customs of the surrounding nations caused Israel to forget God. He became just another god, no better or worse than Baal or Dagon, a Philistine god. Though Israel never fully forgot about God in this time, it's clear that by the end of Judges, their knowledge of Him has been twisted out of shape.

Syncretism will always be a danger to believers of God. In fact, in Revelation we learn that at some point in the future the Antichrist will attempt to unify all world religions into one.

Under the banner of unity and tolerance, the devil, through the Antichrist, will persuade many to join this new world religion. But a mixed and muddied faith is no faith at all. Only those who recognize that Jesus alone is "the way, and the truth, and the life" (John 14:6), will escape the horrors of those days.

How much has changed in your life over the last 22 years? If you're young, the changes have been dramatic. You've been through school, you've grown a lot taller, your features have matured and so have your attitudes. If playing with toy cars was once fun, driving real ones has proven to be a greater experience.

If you're older, say, in your 40s or 50s, the changes are more subtle but still obvious. Your attitudes toward life now involve long-term considerations: paying a mortgage, raising children, preparing for retirement. Driving cars may have once been fun, but now investing in auto makers and other stocks have become a passion. In any event, you are not the same person you were two decades ago.

When reading the Book of Judges, we need to keep in mind the vast number of years flying by us. Otherwise, when you read verses like those referring to the judge Tola, "and he judged

Israel twenty-three years. Then he died" (Judg. 10:2), and then read, "the people of Israel again did what was evil in the sight of the LORD" (10:6), it really sounds like Israel was going from good one day to bad the next. And we scratch our heads wondering how a nation could switch allegiances so quickly.

Well, it wasn't quick. Israel's backsliding took many decades of slowly forgetting God. And that's why the time factor is important. Sometimes Satan attacks suddenly, swiftly, brutally, and we either stand or fall. But one of Satan's deadliest weapons is time and forgetfulness.

The Israelites didn't wake up one morning and decide to reject God. But over years of living so near the Canaanite nations, they eventually turned away from God by adopting pagan practices. Have you ever found yourself tolerating or even accepting something that once made you flinch in disgust? We need to be diligent every day in turning our eyes to God. Daily time in His Word will prevent the erosion of Satan's attacks.

We've seen many times already that though Israel forgot God, God never forgot Israel. That's one reason God sent the foreign armies to oppress Israel—to cause them to cry out for help, to remember God. We see that happening for the sixth time in chapter 10. Again, Israel calls out to God, but this time, God does something different: He calls their bluff.

The people of Israel weren't really repenting of their sins; they were only expressing regret. The difference is that regret is only an emotion, but repentance moves our heart and spurs us to action.

Many people try to "hustle" God into handing out forgiveness. They see praying for forgiveness as a magic spell that automatically wipes away sin. Admitting guilt, and really meaning it, can be one of the hardest things you'll ever do. But then again, admitting sin *shouldn't* be easy. If it were, what would stop us from continually breaking God's commands and destroying the relationship we have with Him?

Over the course of many decades, Israel had forgotten about God. When they did remember Him, Israel tried to hustle God

" Sometimes Satan attacks suddenly, swiftly, brutally, and we either stand or fall. But one of Satan's deadliest weapons is time and forgetfulness. "

with a quick admission of guilt that wasn't accompanied by the acts of true repentance. They actually didn't show repentance until they got rid of their foreign gods (Judg. 10:16). When they destroyed their idols, they found that God "is faithful and just to forgive us our sins and to cleanse us from all unrighteousness" (1 John 1:9).

God doesn't change from year to year, and so this promise still stands. Have you drifted away from your relationship with God? He hasn't forgotten you. He's waiting for you to turn back to Him, repent of your sins and accept His forgiveness. I pray you will.

Express It

If you realized during this lesson that you've been forgetting about God, arrange a reunion. Set aside some time to pray and read your Bible and get reacquainted. As you pray, ask God to show you where you may be compromising your faith in Him. Praise Him for His love and mercy as you ask for forgiveness. Ask for the strength you need to turn away from any sinful habits that are keeping you from drawing near to Him.

Consider It

As you read Judges 10:1–18, consider these questions:

1) In this chapter, Israel turns to different gods. What does this say about the false gods' power to meet their needs?

2) Why does God allow the Philistines and Ammonites to invade?

3) What does God tell Israel the first time they call out to Him?

4) How does Israel respond?

5) What's different this time about how the judge is selected?

6) What's decided about this leader?

7) Why is this difference significant?

Lesson 11

Jephthah—The Tragedy of Ignorance

Though he was a man full of zeal and passion, Jephthah lived in a time when many of God's laws had been forgotten or were mixed up with the pagan culture surrounding Israel. As a result, Jephthah's life, while at times victorious, eventually turned tragic. In this lesson, we'll learn the importance of grounding our faith in God's Word.

Judges 11:1–12:15

Jephthah Delivers Israel

11 Now Jephthah the Gileadite was a mighty warrior, but he was the son of a prostitute. Gilead was the father of Jephthah. ²And Gilead's wife also bore him sons. And when his wife's sons grew up, they drove Jephthah out and said to him, "You shall not have an inheritance in our father's house, for you are the son of another woman." ³Then Jephthah fled from his brothers and lived in the land of Tob, and worthless fellows collected around Jephthah and went out with him.

⁴After a time the Ammonites made war against Israel. ⁵And when the Ammonites made war against Israel, the elders of Gilead went to bring Jephthah from the land of Tob. ⁶And they said to Jephthah, "Come and be our leader, that we may fight with the Ammonites." ⁷But Jephthah said to the elders of Gilead, "Did you not hate me and drive me out of my father's house? Why have you come to me now when you are in distress?" ⁸And the elders of Gilead said to Jephthah, "That is why we have turned to you now, that you may go with us and fight with the Ammonites and be our head over all the inhabitants of Gilead." ⁹Jephthah said to the elders of Gilead, "If you bring me home again to fight with the Ammonites, and the Lord gives them over to me, I will be your head." ¹⁰And the elders of Gilead said to Jephthah, "The Lord will be witness between us, if we do not do as you say." ¹¹So Jephthah went with the elders of Gilead, and the people made him head and leader over them. And Jephthah spoke all his words before the Lord at Mizpah.

¹²Then Jephthah sent messengers to the king of the Ammonites and said, "What do you have against me, that you have come to me to fight against my land?" ¹³And the king of the Ammonites answered the messengers of Jephthah, "Because Israel on coming up from Egypt took away my land, from the Arnon to the Jabbok and to the Jordan; now therefore restore it peaceably." ¹⁴Jephthah again sent messengers to the king of the Ammonites ¹⁵and said to him, "Thus says Jephthah: Israel did not take away the land of Moab or the land of the Ammonites, ¹⁶but when they came up from Egypt, Israel went through the wilderness to the Red Sea and came to Kadesh. ¹⁷Israel then sent messengers to the king of Edom, saying, 'Please let us pass through your land,' but the king of Edom would not listen. And they sent also to the king of Moab, but he would not consent. So Israel remained at Kadesh.

¹⁸"Then they journeyed through the wilderness and went around the land of Edom and the land of Moab and arrived on the east side of the land of Moab and camped on the other side of the Arnon. But they did not enter the territory of Moab, for the Arnon was the boundary of Moab. ¹⁹Israel then sent messengers to Sihon king of the Amorites, king of Heshbon, and Israel said to him, 'Please let us pass through your land to our country,' ²⁰but Sihon did not trust Israel to pass through his territory, so Sihon gathered all his people together and encamped at Jahaz and fought with Israel. ²¹And the Lord, the God of Israel, gave Sihon and all his people into the hand of Israel, and they defeated them. So Israel took possession of all the land of the Amorites, who inhabited that country. ²²And they took possession of all the territory of the Amorites from the Arnon to the Jabbok and from the wilderness to the Jordan. ²³So then the Lord, the God of Israel, dispossessed the Amorites from before his people Israel; and are you to take possession of them? ²⁴Will you not possess what Chemosh your god gives you to possess? And all that the Lord our God has dispossessed before us, we will possess. ²⁵Now

are you any better than Balak the son of Zippor, king of Moab? Did he ever contend against Israel, or did he ever go to war with them? ²⁶While Israel lived in Heshbon and its villages, and in Aroer and its villages, and in all the cities that are on the banks of the Arnon, 300 years, why did you not deliver them within that time? ²⁷I therefore have not sinned against you, and you do me wrong by making war on me. The LORD, the Judge, decide this day between the people of Israel and the people of Ammon." ²⁸But the king of the Ammonites did not listen to the words of Jephthah that he sent to him.

Jephthah's Tragic Vow

²⁹Then the Spirit of the LORD was upon Jephthah, and he passed through Gilead and Manasseh and passed on to Mizpah of Gilead, and from Mizpah of Gilead he passed on to the Ammonites. ³⁰And Jephthah made a vow to the LORD and said, "If you will give the Ammonites into my hand, ³¹then whatever comes out from the doors of my house to meet me when I return in peace from the Ammonites shall be the LORD's, and I will offer it up for a burnt offering." ³²So Jephthah crossed over to the Ammonites to fight against them, and the LORD gave them into his hand. ³³And he struck them from Aroer to the neighborhood of Minnith, twenty cities, and as far as Abel-keramim, with a great blow. So the Ammonites were subdued before the people of Israel.

³⁴Then Jephthah came to his home at Mizpah. And behold, his daughter came out to meet him with tambourines and with dances. She was his only child; beside her he had neither son nor daughter. ³⁵And as soon as he saw her, he tore his clothes and said, "Alas, my daughter! You have brought me very low, and you have become the cause of great trouble to me. For I have opened my mouth to the LORD, and I cannot take back my vow." ³⁶And she said

to him, "My father, you have opened your mouth to the LORD; do to me according to what has gone out of your mouth, now that the LORD has avenged you on your enemies, on the Ammonites." ³⁷So she said to her father, "Let this thing be done for me: leave me alone two months, that I may go up and down on the mountains and weep for my virginity, I and my companions." ³⁸So he said, "Go." Then he sent her away for two months, and she departed, she and her companions, and wept for her virginity on the mountains. ³⁹And at the end of two months, she returned to her father, who did with her according to his vow that he had made. She had never known a man, and it became a custom in Israel ⁴⁰that the daughters of Israel went year by year to lament the daughter of Jephthah the Gileadite four days in the year.

> # Key Verse
>
> And Jephthah made a vow to the LORD and said, "If you will give the Ammonites into my hand, then whatever comes out from the doors of my house to meet me when I return in peace from the Ammonites shall be the LORD's, and I will offer it up for a burnt offering" (Judg. 11:30–31).

Jephthah's Conflict with Ephraim

12 The men of Ephraim were called to arms, and they crossed to Zaphon and said to Jephthah, "Why did you cross over to fight against the Ammonites and did not call us to go with you? We will burn your house over you with fire." ²And Jephthah said to them, "I and my people had a great dispute with the Ammonites, and when I called you, you did not save me from their hand. ³And when I saw that you would not save me, I took my life in my hand and crossed over against the Ammonites, and the LORD gave them into my hand. Why then have you come up to me this day to fight against me?" ⁴Then Jephthah gathered all the men of Gilead and fought with Ephraim. And the men of Gilead struck Ephraim, because they said, "You are fugitives of Ephraim, you Gileadites, in the midst of Ephraim and Manasseh." ⁵And the Gileadites captured the fords of the Jordan against the Ephraimites. And when any of the fugitives of Ephraim said, "Let me go over," the men of Gilead said to him, "Are you an Ephraimite?" When he said, "No," ⁶they said to him, "Then say Shibboleth," and he said, "Sibboleth," for he could not pronounce it right. Then they seized him and slaughtered him at the fords of the Jordan. At that time 42,000 of the Ephraimites fell.

⁷Jephthah judged Israel six years. Then Jephthah the Gileadite died and was buried in his city in Gilead.

Ibzan, Elon, and Abdon

⁸After him Ibzan of Bethlehem judged Israel. ⁹He had thirty sons, and thirty daughters he gave in marriage outside his clan, and thirty daughters he brought in from outside for his sons. And he judged Israel seven years. ¹⁰Then Ibzan died and was buried at Bethlehem.

¹¹After him Elon the Zebulunite judged Israel, and he judged Israel ten years. ¹²Then Elon the Zebulunite died and was buried at Aijalon in the land of Zebulun.

¹³After him Abdon the son of Hillel the Pirathonite judged Israel. ¹⁴He had forty sons and thirty grandsons, who rode on seventy donkeys, and he judged Israel eight years. ¹⁵Then Abdon the son of Hillel the Pirathonite died and was buried at Pirathon in the land of Ephraim, in the hill country of the Amalekites.

Go Deeper

Let's take a moment here to mention some of those judges that don't get talked about too often. The reason is simple—there's just not a lot we know about them. At least with Shamgar, we have a description of an event he was part of.

All of these "obscure" judges occupy the times before and after Jephthah was judge. In Judges 10:1–5, we learn about Tola from the tribe of Issachar who judged Israel for 23 years. He was followed by Jair of Gilead (the land northeast of the Jordan). He was a judge for 22 years. We're also told that he had 30 sons who rode 30 donkeys who governed 30 cities in the land of Gilead.

After Jephthah, we read about Ibzan in Judges 12:8–15 who judged for seven years. He had 30 daughters who were given in marriage to foreign men. Maybe this was an attempt to build political relations, but it was still forbidden by God. Next was Elon who judged for ten

(continued)

Go Deeper Continued . . .

years, and then Abdon who judged for eight years. He had 40 sons and 30 grandsons.

Though their role seems relatively minor, they do fill an important spot in the history of Israel. As Christians, we know there are no minor roles in the kingdom of God. Paul's analogy of the Body of Christ in 1 Corinthians 12:12–26 tells us that though we fill different roles, we all act as one body. Don't be discouraged if you feel your calling isn't as "glamorous" as others. Praise God that He has uniquely equipped you to fill a role no one else could.

Back in Lesson Nine, we saw in the life of Abimelech a man who was ruthless in his quest for power and leadership. Without concern for the Lord's guidance, Abimelech slaughtered the sons of Gideon and proclaimed himself king of Israel. But his "rule" only lasted three years before civil war broke out. The Bible makes it clear that Abimelech's death was God's judgment on him for the way he rose to power.

In many ways Jephthah, the judge in this lesson, was the opposite. Instead of seeking after power and leadership, it was offered to him although, at first glance, Jephthah was an unusual choice for the job.

First of all, Jephthah was an illegitimate child, the result of his father's encounter with a prostitute. Though his father cared for him enough to let Jephthah live in his house, Jephthah's half-brothers drove him away and denied him a share of the family inheritance.

Jephthah went north, to the land of Tob, a place on the frontier of Israel. There he surrounded himself with a sort of mercenary army and formed an unofficial police force that protected the Hebrew people from their enemies. He evidently made a name for himself, because when the leaders of Gilead were looking for someone to lead the fight against the Ammonites, they came to Jephthah.

Now that's a rags-to-riches story. The years Jephthah spent on the frontier taught him many valuable lessons that would benefit him later on. He learned how to fight, he learned leadership, and he learned about God.

Where has God placed you now? Is it a place you enjoy, or are you dreaming of escaping to bigger and better things? One of the lessons of Jephthah is that God never leads anyone anywhere by mistake. Where you are right now is exactly where God wants you and where He'll teach you to be the person He created you to be.

Now there is a difference between being led by God and taking the reins yourself. As we saw with Abimelech, when we take control of our own life the results are often disastrous. But when you allow God control of your life, even the "valley of the shadow of death" (Ps. 23:4) can be a place of blessing. The lessons Jephthah learned in the wilderness were valuable as he made the transition to judge of Israel.

Suddenly, this man who was rejected by his family and forced to live as a mercenary becomes the best man for the job of leading Israel. Our culture praises people who go out and make their own way in the world—the people who set goals and achieve them. God will bless those people as well when they align their goals with God's. But God also uses people like Jephthah, who take each day as it comes, waiting for the day when God will lift them up.

But we also need to talk of Jephthah's deficiency: Jephthah lacked any real understanding of God's character. Though he was passionate for the Lord and His work, his prayer before going into battle, though it sounded noble, was full of mistaken ideas about God and how He works.

"And Jephthah made a vow to the LORD and said, 'If you will give the Ammonites into my hand, then whatever comes out from the doors of my house to meet me when I return in peace from the Ammonites shall be the LORD's, and I will offer it up for a burnt offering'" (Judg. 11:30–31).

Entering into a vow was a very serious proposition. So serious in fact that, though God does allow His people to make vows,

He actually discourages it. (See Eccles. 5:5.) Once made, a vow cannot be broken without destroying the reputation of either of the people involved.

If Jephthah had broken his vow, two things would have happened. One, people wouldn't trust him. He promised something and didn't follow through. Second, because the vow was made to God, failure to fulfill the vow would reflect on God's character. If Jephthah didn't follow through, then, supposedly, the god he vowed to wasn't worth the sacrifice.

Notice also that Jephthah seems to be bargaining with God. "If you'll do this for me, I'll do something for you." The spiritual situation in Israel had gotten to the point where Jephthah thought this was an acceptable way to approach God. But God's not like that at all. He doesn't demand extravagant sacrifices to prove our loyalty. God wants to be our Father, our Friend, and our King. God had promised Israel long ago that He would do great things through the nation and all they had to do to secure God's promise was to listen and obey His Word: The same that any father expects of his child.

The tragedy of Jephthah's life is that he was ignorant of God's character. Though he had great passion for the Lord's work, his incomplete knowledge cost him his only child. As we've seen many times so far in Judges, ignorance leads to tragedy, but knowledge of God is the path to blessing.

Express It

Every day people are falling prey to teachings that sound reasonable but are contrary to everything God stands for. As you pray, ask God to continue to teach you about Himself. As you read His Word, pray that you will learn to love the God of the Scriptures and be able to recognize the false teachings around you.

Consider It

As you read Judges 11:1–12:15, consider these questions:

1) What was the nature of the relationship between Jephthah and his brothers?

2) How did Jephthah respond to the request of the elders?

3) How did Jephthah first approach the Amorites?

4) What happened when Jephthah returned home from the battle?

5) What was Ephraim's complaint against Jephthah?

6) How did Jephthah respond?

7) Describe the three judges after Jephthah.

8) In what way do we see Ibzan ignoring God's law?

Samson—One Man Alone

Among Samson's many faults, one positive trait stands out—he alone in Israel fought against the Philistines. Though his motivations were almost always self-centered, God used Samson to begin Israel's fight against their long-standing enemy, the Philistines. In this lesson, we'll learn the importance of standing even when we stand alone.

Judges 13:1–15:20

The Birth of Samson

13 And the people of Israel again did what was evil in the sight of the Lord, so the Lord gave them into the hand of the Philistines for forty years.

²There was a certain man of Zorah, of the tribe of the Danites, whose name was Manoah. And his wife was barren and had no children. ³And the angel of the Lord appeared to the woman and said to her, "Behold, you are barren and have not borne children, but you shall conceive and bear a son. ⁴Therefore be careful and drink no wine or strong drink, and eat nothing unclean, ⁵for behold, you shall conceive and bear a son. No razor shall come upon his head, for the child shall be a Nazirite to God from the womb, and he shall begin to save Israel from the hand of the Philistines." ⁶Then the woman came and told her husband, "A man of God came to me, and his appearance was like the appearance of the angel of God, very awesome. I did not ask him where he was from, and he did not tell me his name, ⁷but he said to me, 'Behold, you shall conceive and bear a son. So then drink no wine or strong drink, and eat nothing unclean, for the child shall be a Nazirite to God from the womb to the day of his death.'"

⁸Then Manoah prayed to the Lord and said, "O Lord, please let the man of God whom you sent come again to us and teach us what we are to do with the child who will be born." ⁹And God listened to the voice of Manoah, and the angel of God came again to the woman as she sat in the field. But Manoah her husband was not with her. ¹⁰So the woman ran quickly and told her husband, "Behold, the man who came to me the other day has appeared to me." ¹¹And Manoah arose and went after his wife and came to the man and said to him, "Are you the man who spoke to this woman?" And he said, "I am." ¹²And Manoah said, "Now when your words come true, what is to be the child's manner of life, and what is his mission?" ¹³And the angel of the Lord said to Manoah, "Of all that I said to the woman let her be careful. ¹⁴She may not eat of anything that comes from the vine, neither let her drink wine or strong drink, or eat any unclean thing. All that I commanded her let her observe."

¹⁵Manoah said to the angel of the Lord, "Please let us detain you and prepare a young goat for you." ¹⁶And the angel of the Lord said to Manoah, "If you detain me, I will not eat of your food. But if you prepare a burnt offering, then offer it to the Lord." (For Manoah did not know that he was the angel of the Lord.) ¹⁷And Manoah said to the angel of the Lord, "What is your name, so that, when your words come true, we may honor you?" ¹⁸And the angel of the Lord said to him, "Why do you ask my name, seeing it is wonderful?" ¹⁹So Manoah took the young goat with the grain offering, and offered it on the rock to the Lord, to the one who works wonders, and Manoah and his wife were watching. ²⁰And when the flame went up toward heaven from the altar, the angel of the Lord went up in the flame of the altar. Now Manoah and his wife were watching, and they fell on their faces to the ground.

²¹The angel of the Lord appeared no more to Manoah and to his wife. Then Manoah knew that he was the angel of the Lord. ²²And Manoah said to his wife, "We shall surely die, for we have seen God." ²³But his wife said to him, "If the Lord had meant to kill us, he would not have accepted a burnt offering and a grain offering at our hands, or shown us all these things, or now announced to us such things as these." ²⁴And the woman bore a son and called his name Samson. And the young

man grew, and the LORD blessed him. [25]And the Spirit of the LORD began to stir him in Mahaneh-dan, between Zorah and Eshtaol.

Key Verse

And the woman bore a son and called his name Samson. And the young man grew, and the LORD blessed him. And the Spirit of the LORD began to stir him (Judg. 13:24–25).

Samson's Marriage

14 Samson went down to Timnah, and at Timnah he saw one of the daughters of the Philistines. [2]Then he came up and told his father and mother, "I saw one of the daughters of the Philistines at Timnah. Now get her for me as my wife." [3]But his father and mother said to him, "Is there not a woman among the daughters of your relatives, or among all our people, that you must go to take a wife from the uncircumcised Philistines?" But Samson said to his father, "Get her for me, for she is right in my eyes."

[4]His father and mother did not know that it was from the LORD, for he was seeking an opportunity against the Philistines. At that time the Philistines ruled over Israel.

[5]Then Samson went down with his father and mother to Timnah, and they came to the vineyards of Timnah. And behold, a young lion came toward him roaring. [6]Then the Spirit of the LORD rushed upon him, and although he had nothing in his hand, he tore the lion in pieces as one tears a young goat. But he did not tell his father or his mother what he had done. [7]Then he went down and talked with the woman, and she was right in Samson's eyes.

[8]After some days he returned to take her. And he turned aside to see the carcass of the lion, and behold, there was a swarm of bees in the body of the lion, and honey. [9]He scraped it out into his hands and went on, eating as he went. And he came to his father and mother and gave some to them, and they ate. But he did not tell them that he had scraped the honey from the carcass of the lion.

[10]His father went down to the woman, and Samson prepared a feast there, for so the young men used to do. [11]As soon as the people saw him, they brought thirty companions to be with him. [12]And Samson said to them, "Let me now put a riddle to you. If you can tell me what it is, within the seven days of the feast, and find it out, then I will give you thirty linen garments and thirty changes of clothes, [13]but if you cannot tell me what it is, then you shall give me thirty linen garments and thirty changes of clothes." And they said to him, "Put your riddle, that we may hear it." [14]And he said to them,

"Out of the eater came something to eat. Out of the strong came something sweet."

And in three days they could not solve the riddle.

[15]On the fourth day they said to Samson's wife, "Entice your husband to tell us what the riddle is, lest we burn you and your father's house with fire. Have you invited us here to impoverish us?" [16]And Samson's wife wept over him and said, "You only hate me; you do not love me. You have put a riddle to my people, and

you have not told me what it is." And he said to her, "Behold, I have not told my father nor my mother, and shall I tell you?" ¹⁷She wept before him the seven days that their feast lasted, and on the seventh day he told her, because she pressed him hard. Then she told the riddle to her people. ¹⁸And the men of the city said to him on the seventh day before the sun went down,

"What is sweeter than honey?
What is stronger than a lion?"

And he said to them,
"If you had not plowed with my heifer,
you would not have found out my
    riddle."

¹⁹And the Spirit of the LORD rushed upon him, and he went down to Ashkelon and struck down thirty men of the town and took their spoil and gave the garments to those who had told the riddle. In hot anger he went back to his father's house. ²⁰And Samson's wife was given to his companion, who had been his best man.

Samson Defeats the Philistines

15 After some days, at the time of wheat harvest, Samson went to visit his wife with a young goat. And he said, "I will go in to my wife in the chamber." But her father would not allow him to go in. ²And her father said, "I really thought that you utterly hated her, so I gave her to your companion. Is not her younger sister more beautiful than she? Please take her instead." ³And Samson said to them, "This time I shall be innocent in regard to the Philistines, when I do them harm." ⁴So Samson went and caught 300 foxes and took torches. And he turned them tail to tail and put a torch between each pair of tails. ⁵And when he had set fire to the torches, he let the foxes go into the standing grain of the Philistines and set fire to the stacked grain and the standing grain,

as well as the olive orchards. ⁶Then the Philistines said, "Who has done this?" And they said, "Samson, the son-in-law of the Timnite, because he has taken his wife and given her to his companion." And the Philistines came up and burned her and her father with fire. ⁷And Samson said to them, "If this is what you do, I swear I will be avenged on you, and after that I will quit." ⁸And he struck them hip and thigh with a great blow, and he went down and stayed in the cleft of the rock of Etam.

⁹Then the Philistines came up and encamped in Judah and made a raid on Lehi. ¹⁰And the men of Judah said, "Why have you come up against us?" They said, "We have come up to bind Samson, to do to him as he did to us." ¹¹Then 3,000 men of Judah went down to the cleft of the rock of Etam, and said to Samson, "Do you not know that the Philistines are rulers over us? What then is this that you have done to us?" And he said to them, "As they did to me, so have I done to them." ¹²And they said to him, "We have come down to bind you, that we may give you into the hands of the Philistines." And Samson said to them, "Swear to me that you will not attack me yourselves." ¹³They said to him, "No; we will only bind you and give you into their hands. We will surely not kill you." So they bound him with two new ropes and brought him up from the rock.

¹⁴When he came to Lehi, the Philistines came shouting to meet him. Then the Spirit of the LORD rushed upon him, and the ropes that were on his arms became as flax that has caught fire, and his bonds melted off his hands. ¹⁵And he found a fresh jawbone of a donkey, and put out his hand and took it, and with it he struck 1,000 men. ¹⁶And Samson said,

"With the jawbone of a donkey,
    heaps upon heaps,
with the jawbone of a donkey
    have I struck down a thousand men."

¹⁷As soon as he had finished speaking, he threw away the jawbone out of his hand. And that place was called Ramath-lehi.

¹⁸And he was very thirsty, and he called upon the LORD and said, "You have granted this great salvation by the hand of your servant, and shall I now die of thirst and fall into the hands of the uncircumcised?" ¹⁹And God split open the hollow place that is at Lehi, and water came out from it. And when he drank, his spirit returned, and he revived. Therefore the name of it was called En-hakkore; it is at Lehi to this day. ²⁰And he judged Israel in the days of the Philistines twenty years.

Go Deeper

By having his birth announced by the angel of the Lord, Samson joins a very select group in the Bible. In fact, only one other person in the Old Testament had such a distinction, and that was Isaac, the son of Abraham, as told in Genesis 17.

When Abraham was 99 years old, the angel of the Lord came to him and reaffirmed the covenant God had made with Abraham—that Abraham would be the father of many nations. This seemed impossible since Abraham's wife was barren. But a year later, a son was born to Abraham and Sarah. Isaac would be the father of Jacob, and Jacob would have 12 sons which would later become the 12 tribes of Israel.

Though Samson's legacy wasn't as stellar as Isaac's, his work was still important. Samson came at a time when Israel most needed a wake-up call. And though his life was checkered at best, the fight he started would eventually culminate in the kingdom of Israel and the establishing of the line of David which would one day bring the Messiah Himself to earth.

Politically and spiritually speaking, the days of Samson were one of the darkest periods in Israel's history. But if you could have asked the Hebrew people about the health of their nation, they would probably respond, "Things are going great." Why the difference?

Throughout the book of Judges, we've been getting a "God's-eye view" of Israel as a nation. When Israel sins against God, we hear about it. When a judge is raised up to save them, we see clearly that God called the judge. From God's perspective, it is very obvious how sick and depraved the practices of the pagan nations were. And like God, we are left wondering how the people could forget the God that led them out of Egypt.

During this period of about 300 years, we've seen Israel slowly and steadily falling away from God. And when we reach Samson, Israel had almost completely forgotten about God. They had given up living by the laws of Moses. They were living, they thought, peacefully with their foreign neighbors. Buying and selling from them. Giving their sons and daughters in marriage to them. Worshiping the same gods as them. Forgetting that God had forbidden all of this. (See Deut. 7:1–5.)

It's also worth noting that at this time Israel hadn't cried out to God for a deliverer. They had been living under the rule of the Philistines for 40 years and apparently didn't mind. When God raised up Samson, the reason was different. Samson, the angel of the Lord said, would "begin to save Israel from the hand of the Philistines" (Judg. 13:5). Samson would be Israel's wake-up call. Samson would start the fight when no one else even saw an enemy.

Samson was special even before he was born. He was one of the few people in the Bible whose birth was foretold. He was to be a Nazirite, a man set apart to God. A Nazirite was expected to never drink wine or any other strong drink. Samson was also to never touch a dead body. Doing so would make him ritually unclean and unfit for the Lord's service. And, of course, Samson was to never cut his hair. Long hair was the visible sign of a Nazirite. It would be immediately clear to a backsliding Israel that Samson was a man devoted to God.

But even though Samson was a man set apart to God, he was also a slave to his passions. Many times he acted impulsively. When he saw the Philistine woman, he didn't consider whether or not it was right for him to take a foreign wife. He just did it. When he was betrayed to give up the answer to his riddle, he didn't think twice about exacting his revenge in a brutal fashion. But despite his faults, a man like Samson was exactly the kind of person Israel needed at this time. A man full of passion, not willing to accept the status quo, someone willing to take the fight to the Philistines.

We need to be careful, however, not to condone Samson's actions. He was a self-centered man who more often then not acted on his own behalf rather than God's. And even though God worked through Samson, God wasn't endorsing Samson's lifestyle. God would much rather use a person fully committed to serving the Lord. There's no telling how different Samson's life would have turned out if he had given his life fully to God and sought to honor Him with his strength.

Despite his zeal and passion, Samson was a man who fought alone. He's unique among the judges in that he never raised an army, he never rallied the people of Israel to drive out the Philistines. In fact, when a delegation of Philistine leaders came into Israel to capture and execute Samson, the Israelites willingly handed him over. Samson was left to fight off 1,000 Philistine men on his own.

As we said, modern America resembles ancient Israel to an alarming degree. As a result, many faithful Christians find it hard to rally other believers to a godly cause. But if we can take anything away from Samson's life, it's that sometimes we need to start the fight ourselves. But like Samson, we don't fight alone. God is on our side.

Express It

First, make your prayer time the most important part of your day. Ask God to give you a sensitivity to His guiding. Pray that the evil things you may be accepting without knowing it would be shown for what they are. Pray also for the strength to stand up in God's name even if no one stands with you.

Consider It
As you read Judges 13:1–15:20, consider these questions:

1) Who was the visitor who told Manoah and his wife they would have a son?

2) What was their reaction when they learned his identity?

3) What were the requirements of a Nazirite?

4) What ways do you see Samson violating those requirements?

5) When the Philistines chased Samson into Judah, how did the Israelites respond?

6) What does this tell you about their spiritual condition?

7) How does Samson's song after he killed the 1,000 Philistines differ from that of Deborah's?

8) How much time passes between chapters 15 and 16?

Samson— Bittersweet Forgiveness

Samson's pride and arrogance finally caught up with him when he gave in to the pleading of Delilah. Through a lifetime of giving in to temptation, Samson found himself a slave of the enemy. But even in the pit of despair, Samson learned that God will forgive. In this lesson, we'll look at how to avoid temptation and how to face the future as the recipient of God's forgiveness without being haunted by our failures.

Judges 16:1–31

Samson and Delilah

16 Samson went to Gaza, and there he saw a prostitute, and he went in to her. ²The Gazites were told, "Samson has come here." And they surrounded the place and set an ambush for him all night at the gate of the city. They kept quiet all night, saying, "Let us wait till the light of the morning; then we will kill him." ³But Samson lay till midnight, and at midnight he arose and took hold of the doors of the gate of the city and the two posts, and pulled them up, bar and all, and put them on his shoulders and carried them to the top of the hill that is in front of Hebron.

⁴After this he loved a woman in the Valley of Sorek, whose name was Delilah. ⁵And the lords of the Philistines came up to her and said to her, "Seduce him, and see where his great strength lies, and by what means we may overpower him, that we may bind him to humble him. And we will each give you 1,100 pieces of silver." ⁶So Delilah said to Samson, "Please tell me where your great strength lies, and how you might be bound, that one could subdue you."

⁷Samson said to her, "If they bind me with seven fresh bowstrings that have not been dried, then I shall become weak and be like any other man." ⁸Then the lords of the Philistines brought up to her seven fresh bowstrings that had not been dried, and she bound him with them. ⁹Now she had men lying in ambush in an inner chamber. And she said to him, "The Philistines are upon you, Samson!" But he snapped the bowstrings, as a thread of flax snaps when it touches the fire. So the secret of his strength was not known.

¹⁰Then Delilah said to Samson, "Behold, you have mocked me and told me lies. Please tell me how you might be bound."

¹¹And he said to her, "If they bind me with new ropes that have not been used, then I shall become weak and be like any other man." ¹²So Delilah took new ropes and bound him with them and said to him, "The Philistines are upon you, Samson!" And the men lying in ambush were in an inner chamber. But he snapped the ropes off his arms like a thread.

¹³Then Delilah said to Samson, "Until now you have mocked me and told me lies. Tell me how you might be bound." And he said to her, "If you weave the seven locks of my head with the web and fasten it tight with the pin, then I shall become weak and be like any other man." ¹⁴So while he slept, Delilah took the seven locks of his head and wove them into the web. And she made them tight with the pin and said to him, "The Philistines are upon you, Samson!" But he awoke from his sleep and pulled away the pin, the loom, and the web.

¹⁵And she said to him, "How can you say, 'I love you,' when your heart is not with me? You have mocked me these three times, and you have not told me where your great strength lies." ¹⁶And when she pressed him hard with her words day after day, and urged him, his soul was vexed to death. ¹⁷And he told her all his heart, and said to her, "A razor has never come upon my head, for I have been a Nazirite to God from my mother's womb. If my head is shaved, then my strength will leave me, and I shall become weak and be like any other man."

¹⁸When Delilah saw that he had told her all his heart, she sent and called the lords of the Philistines, saying, "Come up again, for he has told me all his heart." Then the lords of the Philistines came up to her and brought the money in their hands. ¹⁹She made him sleep on her knees. And she

called a man and had him shave off the seven locks of his head. Then she began to torment him, and his strength left him. ²⁰And she said, "The Philistines are upon you, Samson!" And he awoke from his sleep and said, "I will go out as at other times and shake myself free." But he did not know that the LORD had left him. ²¹And the Philistines seized him and gouged out his eyes and brought him down to Gaza and bound him with bronze shackles. And he ground at the mill in the prison. ²²But the hair of his head began to grow again after it had been shaved.

The Death of Samson

²³Now the lords of the Philistines gathered to offer a great sacrifice to Dagon their god and to rejoice, and they said, "Our god has given Samson our enemy into our hand." ²⁴And when the people saw him, they praised their god. For they said, "Our god has given our enemy into our hand, the ravager of our country, who has killed many of us." ²⁵And when their hearts were merry, they said, "Call Samson, that he may entertain us." So they called Samson out of the prison, and he entertained them. They made him stand between the pillars. ²⁶And Samson said to the young man who held him by the hand, "Let me feel the pillars on which the house rests, that I may lean against them." ²⁷Now the house was full of men and women. All the lords of the Philistines were there, and on the roof there were about 3,000 men and women, who looked on while Samson entertained.

²⁸Then Samson called to the LORD and said, "O Lord GOD, please remember me and please strengthen me only this once, O God, that I may be avenged on the Philistines for my two eyes." ²⁹And Samson grasped the two middle pillars on which the house rested, and he leaned his weight against them, his right hand on the one and his left hand on the other. ³⁰And Samson said, "Let me die with the Philistines." Then he bowed with all his strength, and the house fell upon the lords and upon all the people who were in it. So the dead whom he killed at his death were more than those whom he had killed during his life. ³¹Then his brothers and all his family came down and took him and brought him up and buried him between Zorah and Eshtaol in the tomb of Manoah his father. He had judged Israel twenty years.

Go Deeper

Some of the most memorable figures in the Bible also experienced some of the greatest failures. Adam and Eve gave in to temptation and ate the forbidden fruit. Abraham lied to the Egyptians because he was afraid they would kill him for his wife. David lied and sent a man to his death to cover up his immoral affair. On the eve of Christ's death, Peter denied even knowing the Savior.

(continued)

Go Deeper Continued . . .

But these events aren't in the Bible as a kind of punishment to these people. In all of these cases, the real story is how God responded to them. And there are a couple of things that are important to learn.

The first is that sin carries consequences. Samson was made a slave. David and Bathsheba lost the child born out of their affair. But the second lesson is that God will forgive when we ask Him. In Psalm 32, David tells us that not

confessing his sin to God wore him down and made it impossible to be happy. But, "I acknowledged my sin to you, and I did not cover my iniquity . . . and you forgave the iniquity of my sin" (v. 5).

Though there are consequences to sin, God has graciously offered to forgive all our sins and spare us from the ultimate result of sin—eternal separation from Him.

Samson is one of the judges that every little boy in Sunday school loves to hear about. Single-handedly, he took on 1,000 Philistines with only a jawbone for a weapon. Earlier, he had taken 300 foxes and sent them through the grain fields dragging torches. And one night in Gaza, he uprooted the city gates and carried them to the top of a hill nearly 40 miles away! But pity the teacher who's asked, "Why was Samson staying the night in Gaza?"

Behind all the amazing feats of daring and strength performed by Samson, we discover a man weak and powerless in the face of temptation. We see a man proud and confident in his abilities, yet not conscious of the fact that his lust was destroying him.

By definition, lust isn't necessarily a bad thing. The word "lust" simply implies a strong feeling. But strong feelings are usually the hardest to control. Imagine a fire hose swinging and flapping wildly under the pressure of the immense amounts of water pouring through it. But then imagine a strong-armed firefighter gaining control of that hose. Suddenly, the fire hose that was useless becomes a valuable tool.

Samson's passions weren't a bad thing in and of themselves; it's just that he had no power over them. Since he was incredibly strong, he often went looking for a fight. He also had a love for women. But without any restrictions on this love, he involved himself with several different women who led him to do incredibly foolish things—Delilah is a case in point.

Passions are good, but uncontrolled passions are dangerous. In Samson's life, this is most clearly evident in his relationship with Delilah.

First, Samson was way "out-of-bounds" in his relationship with Delilah. Besides the fact that he was having a sexual relationship with a woman he wasn't married to, Delilah wasn't an Israelite and was most likely a Philistine, both clear violations of God's commands.

Secondly, Samson toyed with sin rather than running from it. Though Samson didn't take many of his Nazirite vows seriously, he did at least keep his hair uncut. But the first time Delilah asked him about the source of his strength should have also been the last. Samson should have run in the other direction. Instead, Delilah had the opportunity to ask him four times, and the fourth time he told her the truth. The longer you stay in the company of sin, the easier it will be for you to lose control.

Finally, Samson trusted too much in his own strength. Yes, he was a powerful man, maybe the strongest to ever live. But Samson's power didn't come from his hair; it came from God. King David had the right idea when he wrote years later, "Some trust in chariots and some in horses, but we trust in the name of the LORD our God" (Ps. 20:7). When Samson lost sight of God, it wasn't too long until he lost nearly everything else.

But I don't want to end this lesson on Samson without looking at one of the most beautiful verses in this entire book: "But the hair of his head began to grow again after it had been

> *" Passions are good, but uncontrolled passions are dangerous. In Samson's life, this is most clearly evident in his relationship with Delilah. "*

shaved" (Judg. 16:22). God hadn't abandoned Samson. Even though Samson had been brought low by his own sin, God hadn't left him.

Even knowing the correct way to walk before the Lord, sin can overpower us. But never doubt for a moment that God has abandoned you. He loves you too much to leave you lying in the dust. Right now and always He is offering forgiveness. The question is, will you accept it?

Express It

The best way of staying out of temptation is by staying near to God. Make a habit every day of committing your time to the Lord. As you approach each task throughout your day, ask God to help you do it in His name. When you feel yourself starting to lose control, pray that God would renew your strength and help you focus your eyes on Him.

Consider It

As you read Judges 16:1–31, consider these questions:

1) What did Samson do in Gaza?

2) What did the Philistines offer Delilah in return for Samson's secret?

3) How did Delilah finally convince Samson to tell her the source of his strength?

4) What did the Philistines do to Samson when they captured him?

5) How do we know that God forgave Samson?

6) How do we know that Samson had finally turned to God?

7) What happened at the temple of Dagon?

8) How long was Samson judge of Israel?

Eli—Old and Comfortable

Though he was a judge of Israel, Eli lacked any real authority. His sons practiced pagan rituals in the tabernacle right under his nose, and he did little to stop it. Through his life, we'll see the dangers of becoming complacent in our faith.

1 Samuel 2:12–36

Eli's Worthless Sons

[12]Now the sons of Eli were worthless men. They did not know the LORD. [13]The custom of the priests with the people was that when any man offered sacrifice, the priest's servant would come, while the meat was boiling, with a three-pronged fork in his hand, [14]and he would thrust it into the pan or kettle or cauldron or pot. All that the fork brought up the priest would take for himself. This is what they did at Shiloh to all the Israelites who came there. [15]Moreover, before the fat was burned, the priest's servant would come and say to the man who was sacrificing, "Give meat for the priest to roast, for he will not accept boiled meat from you but only raw." [16]And if the man said to him, "Let them burn the fat first, and then take as much as you wish," he would say, "No, you must give it now, and if not, I will take it by force." [17]Thus the sin of the young men was very great in the sight of the LORD, for the men treated the offering of the LORD with contempt.

[18]Samuel was ministering before the LORD, a boy clothed with a linen ephod. [19]And his mother used to make for him a little robe and take it to him each year when she went up with her husband to offer the yearly sacrifice. [20]Then Eli would bless Elkanah and his wife, and say, "May the LORD give you children by this woman for the petition she asked of the LORD." So then they would return to their home.

[21]Indeed the LORD visited Hannah, and she conceived and bore three sons and two daughters. And the young man Samuel grew in the presence of the LORD.

Eli Rebukes His Sons

[22]Now Eli was very old, and he kept hearing all that his sons were doing to all Israel, and how they lay with the women who were serving at the entrance to the tent of meeting. [23]And he said to them, "Why do you do such things? For I hear of your evil dealings from all the people. [24]No, my sons; it is no good report that I hear the people of the LORD spreading abroad. [25]If someone sins against a man, God will mediate for him, but if someone sins against the LORD, who can intercede for him?" But they would not listen to the voice of their father, for it was the will of the LORD to put them to death.

[26]Now the young man Samuel continued to grow both in stature and in favor with the LORD and also with man.

> # Key Verse
>
> Now Eli was very old, and he kept hearing all that his sons were doing to all Israel (1 Sam. 2:22).

The Lord Rejects Eli's Household

[27]And there came a man of God to Eli and said to him, "Thus the LORD has said, 'Did I indeed reveal myself to the house of your father when they were in Egypt subject to the house of Pharaoh? [28]Did I choose him out of all the tribes of Israel to be my priest, to go up to my altar, to burn incense, to wear an ephod before me? I gave to the house of your father all my offerings by fire from the people of Israel. [29]Why then do you scorn my sacrifices and my offerings that I commanded, and honor your sons above me by fattening your-

selves on the choicest parts of every offering of my people Israel?' ³⁰Therefore the LORD the God of Israel declares: 'I promised that your house and the house of your father should go in and out before me forever,' but now the LORD declares: 'Far be it from me, for those who honor me I will honor, and those who despise me shall be lightly esteemed. ³¹Behold, the days are coming when I will cut off your strength and the strength of your father's house, so that there will not be an old man in your house. ³²Then in distress you will look with envious eye on all the prosperity that shall be bestowed on Israel, and there shall not be an old man in your house forever. ³³The only one of you whom I shall not cut off from my altar shall be spared to weep his eyes out to grieve his heart, and all the descendants of your house shall die by the sword of men. ³⁴And this that shall come upon your two sons, Hophni and Phinehas, shall be the sign to you: both of them shall die on the same day. ³⁵And I will raise up for myself a faithful priest, who shall do according to what is in my heart and in my mind. And I will build him a sure house, and he shall go in and out before my anointed forever. ³⁶And everyone who is left in your house shall come to implore him for a piece of silver or a loaf of bread and shall say, "Please put me in one of the priests' places, that I may eat a morsel of bread."'"

Go Deeper

In Eli's life, we see Israel doing something that we didn't see in Samson's life. They were fighting the Philistines. While Samson was alive, he was one man fighting alone while the rest of Israel tried to cope with coexistence. But by the time Eli was growing old, apparently Israel had had enough.

However, the battle we read about in 1 Samuel 4 doesn't go well for Israel. The Philistines win and about 4,000 Israelites die. Something very similar happened years earlier when Israel went up against the city of Ai. There, Israel was defeated because one man had taken items that were to be given to Lord. When Achan confessed and was punished, Israel attacked again and won.

In the days of Eli, the priests of God were committing a similar sin. They were taking the best portions of the sacrifices to God for themselves. And when that sin was taken care of, Israel was able to move forward and deal with their enemies.

Has it felt like your prayers are falling on deaf ears lately? Are you feeling spiritual frustration in your walk with God? Maybe there's something you need to deal with. Pray along with David, "Search me, O God, and know my heart! Try me and know my thoughts! And see if there be any grievous way in me, and lead me in the way everlasting!" (Ps. 139:23–24).

With the death of Samson, we pass out of the book of Judges, but not out of the time of the judges.

Eli represents a kind of person we've seen very little of since the death of Joshua; he was a priest. There are really only a couple of places in Judges where the priests of Israel are mentioned. And both instances show how far from God the priests of the Lord had fallen. When Gideon made the golden ephod, a priestly garment, it's clear that the priests weren't filling their role as ministers to the people. And when the priesthood surfaces again in Judges 17, it's a priesthood for hire and not dedicated to the Lord.

Essentially, in the time of Eli and through the period of the judges, there was no central priesthood. Though the tabernacle of God was established at Shiloh, the ministers of the Lord there had very little influence over the spiritual lives of the Israelites. As it says in Judges 17:6 and 21:25, "In those days there was no king in Israel. Everyone did what was right in his own eyes."

Years later, Solomon would write, "Everyone who is arrogant in heart is an abomination to the LORD; be assured, he will not go unpunished" (Prov. 16:5). Hophni and Phinehas, the sons of Eli, demonstrated this proverb perfectly. The Bible describes these young priests as "worthless men" (1 Sam. 2:12). What a terrible thing to be considered worthless! There was nothing more God could do with them. Though Israel didn't know much about God in those days, they knew enough. They knew it was wrong to conduct pagan rituals in the tabernacle of the Lord (2:22). Because they had devoted their lives to evil, there was nothing more God could do through them. As the proverb promises, they did not go unpunished.

But what about Eli their father, the judge of Israel and priest to the Lord? Where was he while his sons were swindling the people of Israel? It would be one thing if all this happened in secret, and Eli knew nothing about it. But we learn in 1 Samuel 3:13 that Eli knew everything that his sons were doing, yet did nothing to stop it. Only once do we see Eli giving a warning to his sons, but it was only after he was old and his sons had been carrying on their evil practices for years. It was too little too late. Eli had become complacent in his calling, and as a result, he and his sons would die dishonorable deaths.

From Eli we learn, there is no "cruise control" in the Christian life. There is no point where we can say, "I've done enough to serve the Lord," and then coast on into heaven. Every day needs to be a conscious effort to practice the calling that God has given us. Not because God may change His mind about your salvation—that's set for eternity—but because God has a will and purpose for you while you're still on this earth, "plans for wholeness and not for evil, to give you a future and a hope" (Jer. 29:11). Satan wants to take away this future. Even if he's lost your soul to heaven, he'll work day and night to prevent you from knowing the joy that comes from a life dedicated to God.

If the thought of a daily struggle against Satan and his schemes makes you worry, take heart in the words John wrote to all of us: "for he [Jesus]who is in you is greater than he who is in the world" (1 John 4:4). When you make Christ an integral part of your day, you won't have to fight. All you have to do is keep your eyes on Jesus.

Eli's sons had turned their eyes away from God; Eli just turned his eyes away from everything. Here we learn the danger of tolerating sin. The name of God was being mocked and dragged through the dirt by his own sons, and he turned a blind eye to it. Even if Eli didn't participate in the evils of his sons, he became just as guilty as they were by allowing it to continue.

What kinds of sins are you tolerating in your own life? Are there sins you've just grown tired of fighting? Are you listening to music that, while sounding good, is drawing your mind away

" There is no 'cruise control' in the Christian life. There is no point where we can say, 'I've done enough to serve the Lord,' and then coast on into heaven. Every day needs to be a conscious effort to practice the calling which God has given us. "

from God? Put it aside. Are you in a position of authority over someone in a destructive lifestyle? Pray that God would give you the wisdom to know how to act in truth and love. But don't just ignore it.

God hasn't made it hard to follow Him. And Jesus said "my yoke is easy, and my burden is light" (Matt. 11:30). All you have to do is keep your eyes on Jesus.

Express It

Ask God for His help in daily aligning yourself with His will. Pray for guidance in meeting today's decisions with His wisdom. Ask God to keep you from becoming content with where things are and to motivate you to always strive for a deeper relationship with Him.

Consider It

As you read 1 Samuel 2:12–36, consider these questions:

1) What do we learn about Eli's sons in these verses?

_____

_____

_____

2) How does Eli deal with his sons?

_____

_____

_____

3) What is the response of Eli's sons?

_____

_____

_____

4) What is said about Samuel in this passage?

_____

_____

_____

5) According to verse 29, what was the sin of Eli's sons?

_____

_____

_____

6) What does the man of God tell Eli will happen to them?

_____

_____

_____

7) What will be the sign to Eli that the man of God's words will come true?

_____

_____

_____

8) What will God do once Eli and his sons are gone?

_____

_____

_____

Lesson

15

Samuel—Set Apart to God

Samuel, like Samson, was set apart to God from birth. But unlike Samson, Samuel lived a consistent life of service before the Lord. By looking at Samuel's life, we'll see how God can use a person fully committed to following Him and how to live in the world, yet not be part of it.

1 Samuel 1:1–2:11; 3:1–21

The Birth of Samuel

1 There was a certain man of a Ramathaim-zophim of the hill country of Ephraim whose name was Elkanah the son of Jeroham, son of Elihu, son of Tohu, son of Zuph, an Ephrathite. [2]He had two wives. The name of the one was Hannah, and the name of the other, Peninnah. And Peninnah had children, but Hannah had no children.

[3]Now this man used to go up year by year from his city to worship and to sacrifice to the LORD of hosts at Shiloh, where the two sons of Eli, Hophni and Phinehas, were priests of the LORD. [4]On the day when Elkanah sacrificed, he would give portions to Peninnah his wife and to all her sons and daughters. [5]But to Hannah he gave a double portion, because he loved her, though the LORD had closed her womb. [6]And her rival used to provoke her grievously to irritate her, because the LORD had closed her womb. [7]So it went on year by year. As often as she went up to the house of the LORD, she used to provoke her. Therefore Hannah wept and would not eat. [8]And Elkanah, her husband, said to her, "Hannah, why do you weep? And why do you not eat? And why is your heart sad? Am I not more to you than ten sons?"

[9]After they had eaten and drunk in Shiloh, Hannah rose. Now Eli the priest was sitting on the seat beside the doorpost of the temple of the LORD. [10]She was deeply distressed and prayed to the LORD and wept bitterly. [11]And she vowed a vow and said, "O LORD of hosts, if you will indeed look on the affliction of your servant and remember me and not forget your servant, but will give to your servant a son, then I will give him to the LORD all the days of his life, and no razor shall touch his head."

[12]As she continued praying before the LORD, Eli observed her mouth. [13]Hannah was speaking in her heart; only her lips moved, and her voice was not heard. Therefore Eli took her to be a drunken woman. [14]And Eli said to her, "How long will you go on being drunk? Put away your wine from you." [15]But Hannah answered, "No, my lord, I am a woman troubled in spirit. I have drunk neither wine nor strong drink, but I have been pouring out my soul before the LORD. [16]Do not regard your servant as a worthless woman, for all along I have been speaking out of my great anxiety and vexation." [17]Then Eli answered, "Go in peace, and the God of Israel grant your petition that you have made to him." [18]And she said, "Let your servant find favor in your eyes." Then the woman went her way and ate, and her face was no longer sad.

[19]They rose early in the morning and worshiped before the LORD; then they went back to their house at Ramah. And Elkanah knew Hannah his wife, and the LORD remembered her. [20]And in due time Hannah conceived and bore a son, and she called his name Samuel, for she said, "I have asked for him from the LORD."

Samuel Given to the LORD

[21]The man Elkanah and all his house went up to offer to the LORD the yearly sacrifice and to pay his vow. [22]But Hannah did not go up, for she said to her husband, "As soon as the child is weaned, I will bring him, so that he may appear in the presence of the LORD and dwell there forever." [23]Elkanah her husband said to her, "Do what seems best to you; wait until you have weaned him; only, may the LORD establish his word." So the woman remained and nursed her son until she weaned him. [24]And when she had weaned him, she took him up with her, along with a three-year-

old bull, an ephah of flour, and a skin of wine, and she brought him to the house of the Lord at Shiloh. And the child was young. ²⁵Then they slaughtered the bull, and they brought the child to Eli. ²⁶And she said, "Oh, my lord! As you live, my lord, I am the woman who was standing here in your presence, praying to the Lord. ²⁷For this child I prayed, and the Lord has granted me my petition that I made to him. ²⁸Therefore I have lent him to the Lord. As long as he lives, he is lent to the Lord."

And he worshiped the Lord there.

Hannah's Prayer

2 And Hannah prayed and said,

"My heart exults in the Lord;
    my strength is exalted in the Lord.
My mouth derides my enemies,
    because I rejoice in your salvation.
²"There is none holy like the Lord;
    there is none besides you;
    there is no rock like our God.
³Talk no more so very proudly,
    let not arrogance come from your mouth;
for the Lord is a God of knowledge,
    and by him actions are weighed.
⁴The bows of the mighty are broken,
    but the feeble bind on strength.
⁵Those who were full have hired
        themselves out for bread,
    but those who were hungry have ceased
        to hunger.
The barren has borne seven,
    but she who has many children is
        forlorn.
⁶The Lord kills and brings to life;
    he brings down to Sheol and raises up.
⁷The Lord makes poor and makes rich;
    he brings low and he exalts.
⁸He raises up the poor from the dust;
    he lifts the needy from the ash heap
to make them sit with princes
    and inherit a seat of honor.
For the pillars of the earth are the Lord's,
    and on them he has set the world.

⁹"He will guard the feet of his faithful ones,
    but the wicked shall be cut off in
        darkness,
for not by might shall a man prevail.
¹⁰The adversaries of the Lord shall be
        broken to pieces;
    against them he will thunder in heaven.
The Lord will judge the ends of the earth;
    he will give strength to his king
    and exalt the power of his anointed."

¹¹Then Elkanah went home to Ramah. And the boy ministered to the Lord in the presence of Eli the priest.

The Lord Calls Samuel

3 Now the young man Samuel was ministering to the Lord under Eli. And the word of the Lord was rare in those days; there was no frequent vision.

²At that time Eli, whose eyesight had begun to grow dim so that he could not see, was lying down in his own place. ³The lamp of God had not yet gone out, and Samuel was lying down in the temple of the Lord, where the ark of God was.

⁴Then the Lord called Samuel, and he said, "Here I am!" ⁵and ran to Eli and said, "Here I am, for you called me." But he said, "I did not call; lie down again." So he went and lay down.

⁶And the Lord called again, "Samuel!" and Samuel arose and went to Eli and said, "Here I am, for you called me." But he said, "I did not call, my son; lie down again." ⁷Now Samuel did not yet know the Lord, and the word of the Lord had not yet been revealed to him.

⁸And the Lord called Samuel again the third time. And he arose and went to Eli and said, "Here I am, for you called me." Then Eli perceived that the Lord was calling the young man. ⁹Therefore Eli said to Samuel, "Go, lie down, and if he calls you, you shall say, 'Speak, Lord, for your servant

hears.'" So Samuel went and lay down in his place.

¹⁰And the LORD came and stood, calling as at other times, "Samuel! Samuel!" And Samuel said, "Speak, for your servant hears." ¹¹Then the LORD said to Samuel, "Behold, I am about to do a thing in Israel at which the two ears of everyone who hears it will tingle. ¹²On that day I will fulfill against Eli all that I have spoken concerning his house, from beginning to end. ¹³And I declare to him that I am about to punish his house forever, for the iniquity that he knew, because his sons were blaspheming God, and he did not restrain them. ¹⁴Therefore I swear to the house of Eli that the iniquity of Eli's house shall not be atoned for by sacrifice or offering forever."

¹⁵Samuel lay until morning; then he opened the doors of the house of the LORD. And Samuel was afraid to tell the vision to Eli. ¹⁶But Eli called Samuel and said, "Samuel, my son." And he said, "Here I am." ¹⁷And Eli said, "What was it that he told you? Do not hide it from me. May God do so to you and more also if you hide anything from me of all that he told you." ¹⁸So

Samuel told him everything and hid nothing from him. And he said, "It is the LORD. Let him do what seems good to him."

¹⁹And Samuel grew, and the LORD was with him and let none of his words fall to the ground. ²⁰And all Israel from Dan to Beersheba knew that Samuel was established as a prophet of the LORD. ²¹And the Lord appeared again at Shiloh, for the LORD revealed himself to Samuel at Shiloh by the word of the LORD.

Key Verse

And all Israel from Dan to Beersheba knew that Samuel was established as a prophet of the LORD. And the LORD appeared again at Shiloh, for the LORD revealed himself to Samuel at Shiloh by the word of the LORD (1 Sam. 3:20–21).

Go Deeper

Though Samuel is often referred to as the last judge of Israel, this isn't technically true. Before God directed Samuel to anoint Saul as the first king, Samuel made his own sons to be judges in Israel.

Joel and Abijah, Samuel's oldest sons, were appointed judges in Beersheba, a town in southern Israel. But what we read about them in 1 Samuel 8:1–3

shows that they more resembled Eli's sons than their father Samuel. They "did not walk in his [Samuel's] ways but turned aside after gain. They took bribes and perverted justice" (v. 3).

Was Samuel a bad parent? It's hard to say based on what we know. Certainly it's possible that Samuel didn't spend enough time with them teaching them how to walk with the Lord. But it's also

(continued)

Go Deeper Continued . . .

important to remember that we all make our own decisions concerning our relationship with God.

As parents, we need to remember this. And though we can't make the decision for our grown-up children, we can pray for them and take every opportunity to share the love of God with them. After all, God loves them more than we ever could.

There are many striking similarities between Samuel and Samson. Both men were judges of Israel. Both were born to mothers who had been declared barren. And both were set apart to God from before birth. But that's where the similarities end.

Samson went on to live a life that was dedicated to fulfilling his own desires while only barely holding on to what made him distinct as a servant of God. Samson was a Nazirite and, as such, was expected to adhere to certain rules throughout his life. He repeatedly broke all but one of them.

Samuel was also born under a vow. His hair went uncut like Samson's, but his dedication to the Lord went much deeper. When you look at the impact Samuel had in his lifetime, it's tempting to wonder how different Samson's life would have been if he had taken his vows more seriously.

Samuel demonstrates what Samson failed to—life should be lived separated *to* God and not *from* God.

The first way we separate ourselves to God is by separating ourselves from sin. You'd think that growing up in the house of the Lord would be the safest place in the world, the place most removed from sin. But we've already seen that's not the case. Eli, the priest and judge of Israel when Samuel was young, had two sons the Bible describes as "worthless" (1 Sam. 2:12). How did Samuel avoid their corruption?

Perhaps his mother, Hannah, had something to do with it. In contrast to the corruption we see in the house of God, Hannah's prayer after the birth of Samuel showed that she had a heart devoted to God. The end of her prayer proved prophetic: "The adversaries of the LORD shall be broken to pieces; against them he [God] will thunder in heaven" (1 Sam. 2:10).

We separate ourselves from sin for a couple of reasons. The first is because, as believers, sin puts us in danger of discipline. Israel found out over and over that God used the nations around them to discipline them because of their continued sin. God still loved them, but a holy God can't stand idly by while sin festers in the land. God eventually will act—and those actions will not be pleasant.

We also need to separate ourselves from sin because it hinders our usefulness to God. In Ephesians, the apostle Paul writes, "Let all bitterness and wrath and anger and clamor and slander be put away from you, along with all malice" (Eph. 4:31). By doing this, we're allowing God to be a blessing through us to those who need to hear. Paul finishes by saying: "Be kind to one another, tenderhearted, forgiving one another, as God in Christ forgave you" (Eph. 4:32).

We continue to live a life separated to God by separating ourselves from false religious teachers. When Samuel became judge of Israel, he reminded the people of this by saying, "If you are returning to the LORD with all your heart, then put away the foreign gods and the Ashtaroth from among you and direct your heart to the LORD and serve him only" (1 Sam. 7:3).

In Samuel's day, the false teachers were easy to identify because they clearly worshiped a false god. Today, however, there are many people who claim to be Christians but teach false doctrine. John gives us this advice: "Beloved, do not believe every spirit, but test the spirits to see whether they are from God, for many false prophets have gone out into the world" (1 John 4:1). Do these so-called Christians recognize the lordship of Christ? If not, walk on.

Finally, being separated to God is a positive thing. Samuel found out that God gives strength to those who separate themselves to Him. Though he didn't have physical strength like

> **"*A holy God can't stand idly by while sin festers in the land. God eventually will act—and those actions will not be pleasant.*"**

Samson, as Samuel grew in the Lord, he became a respected man. Everyone in Israel knew about Samuel and his special relationship with God. As Samuel's mother prayed, "He [God] raises up the poor from the dust . . . to make them sit with princes and inherit a seat of honor" (1 Sam. 2:8).

Living a life separated to God will be difficult, and people often take the idea to one of two extremes. They will either separate themselves so much that they can no longer share the love of Christ with others, or they don't separate enough and find themselves indistinguishable from the people they are trying to reach.

Ultimately our example of a separated life is Jesus. Though we learn a lot from Samuel, Jesus was the epitome of living a separated, yet not isolated, life. A life devoted to God but not removed from the people He came to reach. Only by drawing near to Jesus will we be able to find that balance in our own lives.

Express It

As you pray today, ask God to show you where the balance is between living in the world yet set apart to God. Pray for wisdom in discerning what things in your life are actually drawing you away from God's love. Pray that you will experience the joy that comes from being a servant of God.

Consider It

As you read 1 Samuel 1:1–2:11; 3:1–21, consider these questions:

1) How did Elkanah's other wife treat Hannah?

_____

_____

2) How do you react when others treat you badly?

_____

_____

_____

3) How did Hannah react?

_____

_____

4) What do we learn about God and those He uses from Hannah's prayer in chapter 2?

_____

_____

_____

5) What examples of this have you seen in your own life?

_____

_____

_____

6) What was God's message to Samuel?

_____

_____

_____

7) How can we avoid the fate of Eli?

_____

_____

_____

8) How does God bless Samuel?

_____

_____

_____

Samuel— Anointing of a King

With Samuel and his sons, the line of judges ends. When Saul was anointed king, all authority over Israel was placed in one man. But as Samuel reminds the people, this one man was squarely under the authority of God. Though today in America we live in a democracy, we also live in a spiritual monarchy with God on the throne. In this lesson, we'll learn how to experience joy and fulfillment in serving our King.

1 Samuel 7:1–8:22; 12:1–25

7 And the men of Kiriath-jearim came and took up the ark of the LORD and brought it to the house of Abinadab on the hill. And they consecrated his son Eleazar to have charge of the ark of the LORD. ²From the day that the ark was lodged at Kiriath-jearim, a long time passed, some twenty years, and all the house of Israel lamented after the LORD.

Samuel Judges Israel

³And Samuel said to all the house of Israel, "If you are returning to the LORD with all your heart, then put away the foreign gods and the Ashtaroth from among you and direct your heart to the LORD and serve him only, and he will deliver you out of the hand of the Philistines." ⁴So the people of Israel put away the Baals and the Ashtaroth, and they served the LORD only.

⁵Then Samuel said, "Gather all Israel at Mizpah, and I will pray to the LORD for you." ⁶So they gathered at Mizpah and drew water and poured it out before the LORD and fasted on that day and said there, "We have sinned against the LORD." And Samuel judged the people of Israel at Mizpah. ⁷Now when the Philistines heard that the people of Israel had gathered at Mizpah, the lords of the Philistines went up against Israel. And when the people of Israel heard of it, they were afraid of the Philistines. ⁸And the people of Israel said to Samuel, "Do not cease to cry out to the LORD our God for us, that he may save us from the hand of the Philistines." ⁹So Samuel took a nursing lamb and offered it as a whole burnt offering to the LORD. And Samuel cried out to the LORD for Israel, and the LORD answered him. ¹⁰As Samuel was offering up the burnt offering, the Philistines drew near to attack Israel. But the LORD thundered with a mighty sound that day against the Philistines and threw them into confusion, and they were routed before Israel. ¹¹And the men of Israel went out from Mizpah and pursued the Philistines and struck them, as far as below Beth-car.

¹²Then Samuel took a stone and set it up between Mizpah and Shen and called its name Ebenezer; for he said, "Till now the LORD has helped us." ¹³So the Philistines were subdued and did not again enter the territory of Israel. And the hand of the LORD was against the Philistines all the days of Samuel. ¹⁴The cities that the Philistines had taken from Israel were restored to Israel, from Ekron to Gath, and Israel delivered their territory from the hand of the Philistines. There was peace also between Israel and the Amorites.

¹⁵Samuel judged Israel all the days of his life. ¹⁶And he went on a circuit year by year to Bethel, Gilgal, and Mizpah. And he judged Israel in all these places. ¹⁷Then he would return to Ramah, for his home was there, and there also he judged Israel. And he built there an altar to the LORD.

Israel Demands a King

8 When Samuel became old, he made his sons judges over Israel. ²The name of his firstborn son was Joel, and the name of his second, Abijah; they were judges in Beersheba. ³Yet his sons did not walk in his ways but turned aside after gain. They took bribes and perverted justice.

⁴Then all the elders of Israel gathered together and came to Samuel at Ramah ⁵and said to him, "Behold, you are old and your sons do not walk in your ways. Now appoint for us a king to judge us like all the nations." ⁶But the thing displeased Samuel when they said, "Give us a king to judge us." And Samuel prayed to the LORD. ⁷And the LORD said to Samuel, "Obey the voice of the people in all that they say to

you, for they have not rejected you, but they have rejected me from being king over them. [8]According to all the deeds that they have done, from the day I brought them up out of Egypt even to this day, forsaking me and serving other gods, so they are also doing to you. [9]Now then, obey their voice; only you shall solemnly warn them and show them the ways of the king who shall reign over them."

Samuel's Warning Against Kings

[10]So Samuel told all the words of the LORD to the people who were asking for a king from him. [11]He said, "These will be the ways of the king who will reign over you: he will take your sons and appoint them to his chariots and to be his horsemen and to run before his chariots. [12]And he will appoint for himself commanders of thousands and commanders of fifties, and some to plow his ground and to reap his harvest, and to make his implements of war and the equipment of his chariots. [13]He will take your daughters to be perfumers and cooks and bakers. [14]He will take the best of your fields and vineyards and olive orchards and give them to his servants. [15]He will take the tenth of your grain and of your vineyards and give it to his officers and to his servants. [16]He will take your male servants and female servants and the best of your young men and your donkeys, and put them to his work. [17]He will take the tenth of your flocks, and you shall be his slaves. [18]And in that day you will cry out because of your king, whom you have chosen for yourselves, but the LORD will not answer you in that day."

The LORD Grants Israel's Request

[19]But the people refused to obey the voice of Samuel. And they said, "No! But there shall be a king over us, [20]that we also may be like all the nations, and that our king may judge us and go out before us and fight our battles." [21]And when Samuel had heard all the words of the peo-

ple, he repeated them in the ears of the LORD. [22]And the LORD said to Samuel, "Obey their voice and make them a king." Samuel then said to the men of Israel, "Go every man to his city."

Samuel's Farewell Address

12 And Samuel said to all Israel, "Behold, I have obeyed your voice in all that you have said to me and have made a king over you. [2]And now, behold, the king walks before you, and I am old and gray; and behold, my sons are with you. I have walked before you from my youth until this day. [3]Here I am; testify against me before the LORD and before his anointed. Whose ox have I taken? Or whose donkey have I taken? Or whom have I defrauded? Whom have I oppressed? Or from whose hand have I taken a bribe to blind my eyes with it? Testify against me and I will restore it to you." [4]They said, "You have not defrauded us or oppressed us or taken anything from any man's hand." [5]And he said to them, "The LORD is witness against you, and his anointed is witness this day, that you have not found anything in my hand." And they said, "He is witness."

[6]And Samuel said to the people, "The LORD is witness, who appointed Moses and Aaron and brought your fathers up out of the land of Egypt. [7]Now therefore stand still that I may plead with you before the LORD concerning all the righteous deeds of the LORD that he performed for you and for your fathers. [8]When Jacob went into Egypt, and the Egyptians oppressed them, then your fathers cried out to the LORD and the LORD sent Moses and Aaron, who brought your fathers out of Egypt and made them dwell in this place. [9]But they forgot the LORD their God. And he sold them into the hand of Sisera, commander of the army of Hazor, and into the hand of the Philistines, and into the hand of the king of Moab. And they fought against them. [10]And they cried out to the LORD and said, 'We have sinned,

because we have forsaken the LORD and have served the Baals and the Ashtaroth. But now deliver us out of the hand of our enemies, that we may serve you.' ¹¹And the LORD sent Jerubbaal and Barak and Jephthah and Samuel and delivered you out of the hand of your enemies on every side, and you lived in safety. ¹²And when you saw that Nahash the king of the Ammonites came against you, you said to me, 'No, but a king shall reign over us,' when the LORD your God was your king. ¹³And now behold the king whom you have chosen, for whom you have asked; behold, the LORD has set a king over you. ¹⁴If you will fear the LORD and serve him and obey his voice and not rebel against the commandment of the LORD, and if both you and the king who reigns over you will follow the LORD your God, it will be well. ¹⁵But if you will not obey the voice of the LORD, but rebel against the commandment of the LORD, then the hand of the LORD will be against you and your king. ¹⁶Now therefore stand still and see this great thing that the LORD will do before your eyes. ¹⁷Is it not wheat harvest today? I will call upon the LORD, that he may send thunder and rain. And you shall know and see that your wickedness is great, which you have done in the sight of the LORD, in asking for yourselves a king." ¹⁸So Samuel called upon the LORD, and the LORD sent thunder and rain that day, and all the people greatly feared the LORD and Samuel.

¹⁹And all the people said to Samuel, "Pray for your servants to the LORD your God, that we may not die, for we have added to all

Key Verse

"If you will fear the LORD and serve him and obey his voice and not rebel against the commandment of the LORD, and if both you and the king who reigns over you will follow the LORD your God, it will be well" (1 Sam. 12:14).

our sins this evil, to ask for ourselves a king." ²⁰And Samuel said to the people, "Do not be afraid; you have done all this evil. Yet do not turn aside from following the LORD, but serve the LORD with all your heart. ²¹And do not turn aside after empty things that cannot profit or deliver, for they are empty. ²²For the LORD will not forsake his people, for his great name's sake, because it has pleased the LORD to make you a people for himself. ²³Moreover, as for me, far be it from me that I should sin against the LORD by ceasing to pray for you, and I will instruct you in the good and the right way. ²⁴Only fear the LORD and serve him faithfully with all your heart. For consider what great things he has done for you. ²⁵But if you still do wickedly, you shall be swept away, both you and your king."

Go Deeper

Though the king was the leader of the people, he was still responsible to live under the authority of God. Saul, the first king of Israel, sometimes forgot this. In one of his first battles against the Philistines, Saul was instructed to wait for Samuel who would come and offer a sacrifice to the Lord after seven

(continued)

Go Deeper Continued . . .

days. On the seventh day, Saul grew impatient and took matters into his own hands. When Samuel arrived soon after, he declared that Saul's kingdom would end with him—he would have no son on the throne (1 Sam. 13:8–14).

Later, Saul again overstepped his authority by refusing to carry out God's command to the letter. As a result, Samuel told Saul that God had rejected him as king (15:1–35).

Someone has said, "As a leader goes, so go his or her followers." This is especially important for leaders in the church. In the New Testament, Paul stresses the importance for the church leaders to live blameless lives before the Lord. (See 1 Tim. 3.) Though we are all responsible for our own choices, we often learn by example. What kind of example are you setting in your church or family?

From a purely sociological perspective, the Scripture reading for this lesson can seem a bit puzzling, specifically the part where the people realize it was a sin to ask for a king. Isn't establishing a kingdom a good thing?

Up to this point, Israel had been a fairly loose group of tribes sharing a common ancestry. But a king would centralize the government. Israel would be able to have a standing army. It would be able to establish trade with other nations and increase its wealth, size and power. In looking at the example of other nations, moving from a congregation of tribes to a centralized government would be a very positive move.

But that's exactly why it was the wrong move. Israel wasn't supposed to look like other nations. When Samuel was old and the future uncertain, the elders approached him and said, "Now appoint for us a king to judge us like all the nations" (1 Sam. 8:5). This was partly spurred by the fact that Samuel's sons were terrible judges. They were corrupt and didn't care about justice (8:3).

While Samuel was judge, the Philistines were driven out of much of the land and were generally not a problem. Earlier in his life, Samuel led the entire nation to repentance. As a result, the people of Israel destroyed their idols and turned to worship God (7:4).

In one of his final addresses to the people of Israel, Samuel reminded the people of their history. He reminded them of Aaron and Moses and how God brought them out of Egypt in a miraculous way. And he reminded them of the foreign nations who oppressed Israel and how God raised up judges to save them when they cried out to God. Whenever Israel was in trouble and called to God, He was not slow to save them. In the days that Israel followed after God, the people were prosperous and had many years of peace.

Most telling, however, is how Samuel started his address. He asked the Israelites if he, Samuel, had ever taken anything from the Israelites. Had he ever demanded payment for anything? Had he ever cheated them out of anything? They answered with a resounding, "No."

A king would be different, though. A man responsible for building a national identity would require many things to accomplish this purpose. In 1 Samuel 8:10–18, Samuel told the people exactly what a king would cost them. A king would take the best of the crops and the livestock. He would draft the young men into his army. The people's daughters would be servants in the king's household. If Samuel had cost them nothing, a king would cost them everything.

What the people realized after the fact was that a human king was completely unnecessary. Though the past 300 years weren't exactly perfect, when they looked to God, He performed all the functions of a king. They didn't need a standing army when God was fighting for them (7:10). Israel didn't need a king to lead them into battle. God was always faithful to raise up a judge in the past. They didn't need foreign trade to bring in food and wealth; God gave them a land that flowed with milk and honey.

Today, even though the times are different, our God is the same. We as Christians don't fight wars against armies like the people of Israel did, but we fight spiritual battles every day. And

> **"***There is no template for the perfect servant of God. Anyone from anywhere, no matter their skills or background, is capable of witnessing great and mighty acts of God.***"**

yes, we stumble many times. Satan will use these times to try and convince us that we're a failure. "Let someone else fight," he'll say. "You're a loser."

But Samuel's message to Israel thousands of years ago is God's message to you today: "Do not be afraid; you have done all this evil. Yet do not turn aside from following the Lord, but serve the Lord with all your heart. . . . For the Lord will not forsake his people, for his great name's sake, because it has pleased the Lord to make you a people for himself" (12:20, 22).

We've seen in the lives of the judges that there is no template for the perfect servant of God. Anyone from anywhere, no matter their skills or background, is capable of witnessing great and mighty acts of God. You have a King in heaven ready to use you in ways you never thought possible. Let God sit on the throne of your life, and you'll never have the need for another.

Express It

Have there been other people or places you've been turning to for help in your life? Try giving your concerns to God, and see how He responds. Let Him know that you trust Him alone, and find some way to demonstrate that trust. Ask God to help you find the joy and fulfillment that comes from being in His service.

Consider It

As you read 1 Samuel 7:1–8:22; 12:1–25, consider these questions:

1) What was the reaction of the Israelites at Mizpah when they heard about the Philistines?

2) What did they ask Samuel to do?

3) What is the significance of the stone Samuel sets up after the battle?

4) What prompts the elders to ask for a king?

5) In what ways, if any, have you found yourself looking for a new king?

6) What sign does God give to the people during Samuel's last address?

7) How do they respond?

8) Samuel agrees to pray for Israel despite their implicit rejection of him. Would you be able to do the same thing? Why or why not?

Notes